Country Crafts

Valerie Janitch

Country Crafts

Ordinary wooden mixing spoons are trimmed with everlasting flowers as a modern wall decoration which anyone can make.

A Studio Book

The Viking Press · New York

Originally published in England under the title of
Handmade at Home

Copyright © 1973 by Valerie Janitch

All rights reserved

Published in 1973 by The Viking Press, Inc.
625 Madison Avenue, New York, N.Y. 10022

Published simultaneously in Canada by
The Macmillan Company of Canada Limited

SBN 670–24419–8

Library of Congress catalog card number: 73–6079

Printed and bound in England

Contents

PREFACE   7

1 COUNTRY HARVEST   9
    Baby owl collage using natural materials; Autumn
    cascade table decoration; country housewife
    paper figures.

2 OUT OF THE ORCHARD—AND INTO THE
  KITCHEN   22
    Country bonnet peaches; wooden spoon wall
    decorations; "Summer" collage using dried
    vegetables and string; dainty eggs for Easter;
    Hallowe'en apple witches.

3 FLOWERS WITH A FUTURE   30
    Preserving flowers and foliage; statice pomander
    balls; a boxful of flowers; evergreen candle
    branch.

4 PICTURE IT IN FLOWERS   43
    How to make pictures using dried flowers and
    foliage—"After the harvest"; "Straw-daisy
    circlet"; "October blaze"; "Springtime";
    "Meadowsweet".

5 LIGHTING-UP TIME   49
    Five lamps and matching shades to make;
    decorating cheap candles to look expensive;
    unusual candle-stands; a honeycomb candle to
    make.

6 WEAR IT COUNTRY STYLE   63
    Seven casual belts with jewellery to match.

7 VICTORIAN ECHOES   73
    Miniature bell jars; antique "silver" cross;
    "pewter" horseshoe flower frame; pottery
    candlestick; "china" bells; velvet book-mark;
    roses and forget-me-nots paperweight; the
    scents of summer—pot-pourri perfume jar and
    lavender sachets.

8 CHRISTMAS IS COMING . . .   87
    Greetings cards for all occasions; "Once in royal
    David's city . . ." Nativity scene.

Preface

This book is intended for everyone who either enjoys making things, or has ever thought they would like the creative satisfaction of making something. And it is specially for anyone who shares my love of the countryside but, for practical reasons, has to live nearer the city than green fields. Although many of the materials can be found in their natural surroundings—gardens, fields and hedgerows—everything can also be bought in towns and cities—and much of it is "faked"! So even if your nearest blade of grass is in the local park, you can still make anything you choose from this miscellany of items which I have designed to evoke the peace and beauty of living in the country in all its seasons.

For the inexperienced, I have given detailed and explicit directions for the various items as I have made them and as they appear in the illustrations. But I have also made it clear how you can, if you wish, adapt everything—substituting your own materials and ideas to interpret my basic designs in your own individual way.

Finally, I hope that the things I have designed throughout this book will give pleasure when they are *finished*, too: whether in use, or wear—or purely as an ornament or decoration about the home. And I hope you will find some useful ideas for original gifts with a really personal touch.

Materials

Bear in mind

If you can't get the dried materials you want from your local florist—don't be afraid to press for them. There's a lot of money in ready-made decorations, and many florists prefer to sell grasses and flowers only in this form. So don't be put off too easily: you could well be pioneering a supply for other, more timid enthusiasts! But if you're drying your own grasses, do remember to cut the seed-heads *before* they are fully ripe —otherwise they will tend to drop: see chapter 3 for full details.

As for the country housewives. . . . I'm rather proud of my invented maize leaves! They just prove how it is possible to fake an effect, if you continue to bear in mind the appearance of the original you are trying to imitate. Plastic generally tends always to look like plastic, so I try to avoid it—but it's amazing how it is possible to make one basically natural material resemble another . . . like the poster-coloured crêpe paper and the stranded embroidery cotton "hair".

1 *Country Harvest*

Whether or not they are the genuine gleanings of a country walk in late summer, the sun-ripened fruits of field and hedgerow provide inspiring material for imaginative decorations in the home. But—as you will discover throughout this book—if I can't find the real thing, I don't hesitate to cheat. Whether it's just a case of buying dyed grasses from a florist, or treating crêpe paper to resemble maize leaves, it's the end product that matters. If I achieve the effect I want to create, and I am satisfied that the finished article has charm, my conscience is clear!

Take the baby owl, for example: an almost three-dimensional collage on a rough hessian ground. I saw a bunch of brown feathery grass in a London store, and it immediately suggested the soft down of a young bird. I added another type of dyed grass, with coarser seed-heads, for the wings—and couldn't resist the soft, short, creamy-brown heads which make his fluffy chest and tufty ears. The advantage of buying bunches like this is that gradually one forms a collection—which contributes to all kinds of other things. In the meantime, the "left-overs" make spectacular arrangements around the house as they await another call to duty. Look at the cascading table decoration—then look again at the owl: you'll find you can play "spot the same materials" throughout the book!

The light, feathery grass above the owl's beak, I found in a field. The honesty petals and everlasting straw-daisies (helichrysums) which make his wide-awake eyes were grown in my own garden (they're *very* easy—and fun—to grow): I pinched his beak from a plate of walnuts before the rest were eaten— and picked his conker feet up under a horse-chestnut tree in the park. His cork bark branch came from a florist—but could easily be a thick twig—and I bought a generous packet of bay leaves from my grocer.

9

Baby owl collage

So if you're a purist, you won't approve of my baby owl: but that needn't stop you doing a similar collage of your own, using dried grass seed-heads and other materials, all of which you have picked, found or grown yourself. That way you'll have an even more satisfying result to display with pride. (You will find notes on drying your own flowers and foliage in Chapter 3.) But *my* collage is proof to city-dwellers that they can create natural-looking decorations just as easily as their country cousins.

This is how I developed my baby owl in his leafy setting. Follow my example as much or as little as you wish.

Method

Trim the card evenly and make sure the corners are right-angles. Then spread thickly with wallpaper paste, and press the hessian down smoothly on top. When dry, bind each side with adhesive tape.

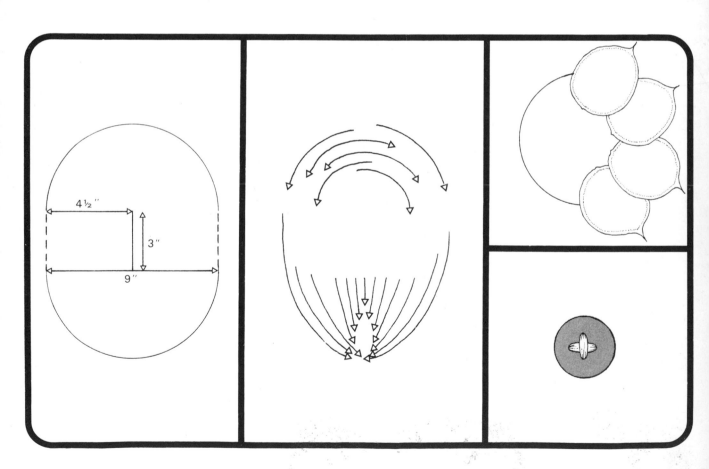

Materials

Brown, feathery grass for body

Coarser brown grass for wings

Fluffy, creamy-brown grass heads for chest

Light, feathery grass above beak

Honesty petals

Straw-daisies (helichrysums) for eyes

Walnut-half for beak

Chestnuts for feet

Cork bark or thick twig

Bay leaves or preserved leaves

A piece of heavy card 22 ins. by 16 ins.

Unbleached hessian the same size

$2\frac{1}{4}$ yds. $\frac{1}{2}$-in.-wide braid for frame

Wallpaper paste

Clear all-purpose adhesive

Double-sided clear tape

Strong adhesive tape

$\frac{1}{2}$-in. steel pins

Adhesive tabs or rings to hang

On a piece of paper at least 12 ins. deep by 9 ins. wide, rule a 3-in. vertical line. With the point of your compasses at each end of the line, and a radius of $4\frac{1}{2}$ ins., draw 9-in.-diameter semi-circles as in diagram 1, joining each side as indicated by the broken lines. Cut out and place this pattern on your hessian, $4\frac{1}{2}$ ins. from the top, with $5\frac{1}{2}$ ins. clear underneath and 3 ins at each side. Draw round it.

Now begin to work out the composition of your owl. I used four 6-to-8-in. grass-heads for each wing, assembling them in position while I decided the arrangement of the feathery grass for the body. Having seen the effect of the body grass against the wings, I was able to stick the wing grass-heads (beginning at the inside, and using clear all-purpose adhesive) so that the tops would be hidden by the body grass. This I stuck down in sections, gradually making them smaller by breaking off just the amount I needed to fill in the shape. You can see in the diagram how I began at each side of the outline, working down towards the centre, and then finishing across the top, with pieces going in both directions.

Mark a point 4 ins. below the top of his head for the beak. Beginning at the lower edge of the chest, stick grass-heads in layers up to the level of the beak (following the illustration for the shape). Stick a tuft of grass-heads so that they will fan out above the beak, as shown.

To make up each eye, cut out a $2\frac{3}{4}$-in.-diameter circle of tissue paper. Stick honesty petals (about eight) to the paper, overlapping each other and extending about $\frac{1}{4}$ in. over the outer edge of the circle (making the completed circle about $3\frac{1}{4}$ ins. wide—see diagram). Stick the two circles at each side of the beak marking, about $\frac{1}{2}$ in. apart. Now stick the beak into position, followed by a straw-daisy for each eye (anchor these with pins, hidden in the petals, if necessary). Stick ears and feet into place (securing the latter with pins from the back of the card). A good alternative eye, if you can't find any suitable dried flowers, is a dark wooden button, the centre picked out in natural raffia (see diagram).

Stick and pin the bark just below his feet and then arrange leaves above and below, fixing them in position with double-sided tape.

If you want to stiffen the picture and add weight, tape another piece of card behind the first. Then stick braid round the edge and fix tabs or rings at the back to hang.

Autumn cascade

A collection of bleached seed-heads, falling away from a tall central ear of barley, suggests the ripe cornfields at harvest-time, and makes a striking display—ideal for a dim corner, or against a dark wall. I set off the creamy monotone of the decoration with a wooden egg cup, but almost any kind of base could be effective: a heavy, glazed pottery egg cup or candle base, an earthenware butter pat—or a tall, ornate gilt candlestick.

It is one of the sorrows of my life that I am not clever with fresh flowers: I *can't* make them do what I want them to! But the joy of working with dried materials in an arrangement like this, is that you stick them in—and there they stay . . . for months, if you like! They won't wilt or die, and they're sturdy enough to stand up to quite rough treatment. The secret of this particular piece is to break the seed-heads up into short sections, poking each bit in separately.

As before, you are free to make your own choice of materials, either finding or buying those which appeal to you. Here is my own selection: as usual, a collection of purchased, found and home-grown.

Table decoration

Materials

A barley head
Dried field grass seed-
heads
Bleached oats
Bleached feathery grass
Heavier fluffy heads (as
owl's chest)
Cream straw-daisies
(helichrysums)
A wooden egg cup or
alternative (see above)
Stone-coloured plasticine
(or white)
A thin rod (a garden
stake, broken knitting
needle, etc.), about 4
ins. Long
Pins

Method

Roll some plasticine into a ball and press it down into the bowl of the egg cup or base you are using: add more, if necessary, to fill it, with a small mound above. Push the rod right down to the base, then turn it to check the rod is absolutely straight. Now use more plasticine to build up above the base, moulding it round the rod, as shown in the diagram, tapering slightly towards the top. Re-check that it is still straight from all angles.

Cut the barley stalk about 4 ins. below the head, then push it down into the top of the plasticine so that the overall height, from the *top* of the egg cup, is about 9 ins. (not including the whiskers!). Now begin to surround the barley with delicate grass-heads cutting them about 5–6 ins. long, and pushing the stalks down into the plasticine.

Continue to circle the plasticine with oats, and then a selection of grass seed-heads, growing heavier and protruding at a wider angle as you progress downwards: the widest point should measure about 9 ins. across.

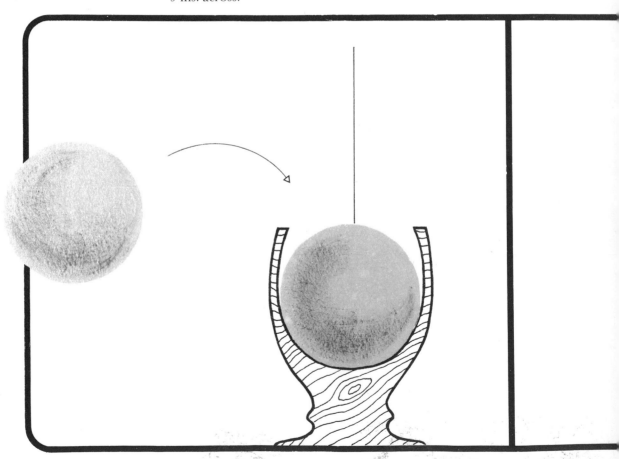

14

Fill in with more heads, to hide any visible plasticine, and finally encircle the top of the base closely with straw-daisy heads (or other dried flowers): fix these with a pin stuck through the centre of the flower, the head pushed right down so that it is buried invisibly.

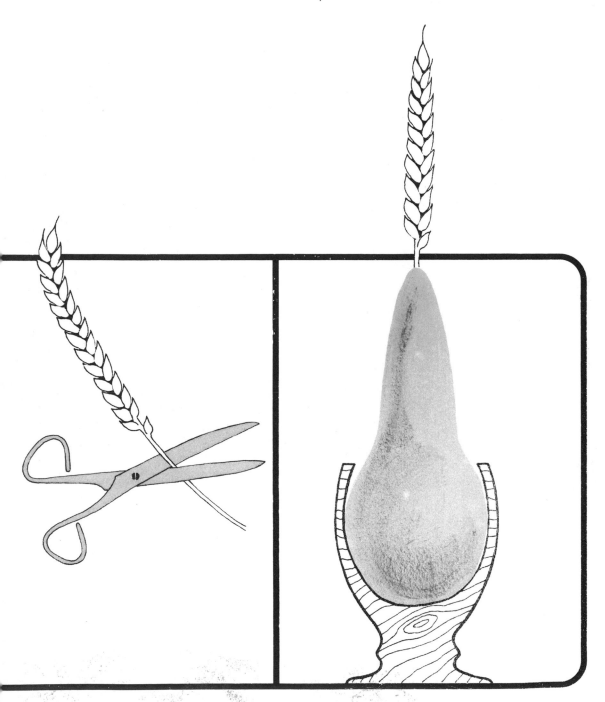

Country housewife

paper figures   For centuries, from the last sheaf to be cut, British harvest workers plaited and wove straws of corn into skilful and elaborate arrangements called "corn dollies", which later played an important part in the harvest home celebrations. But only some of the traditional shapes vaguely resemble a human figure, and it is likely that "dolly" is simply a derivation of idol.

But in the United States, the corn dolly tradition is perpetuated in attractive little housewife figures made from the outer leaves of the ripe maize husk, with the "silk" found inside the ear of corn used for hair. Often a mother carries a babe-in-arms, made in the same way. The American Indians, too, make similar figures—dressed in Red Indian style. And in Czechoslovakia, cottagers make delightful little peasant figures very like the American ones, busily occupied in all manner of household duties.

I thought the American and Czech figures so charming that I determined to make my own "corn dollies". My problem was the maize! The nearest I could get was the protective leaves round the corn-on-the-cob: but this wasn't very practical, because greengrocers remove most of the leaf . . . and corn-on-the-cob isn't in season for long—the rest of the year sweet corn comes in cans! Crêpe paper seemed to be the answer, the grain and texture of the paper resembling the real thing very well. However, I couldn't buy corn or maize-coloured crêpe—so I had to colour my own.

After much experiment—which included crayons, tea-bags, coffee, linseed oil and beeswax—I found poster paint by far the most successful method, and well worth the trouble. I diluted white poster colour in a saucer, then added a little colour at a time until I achieved the creamy-yellow shade I wanted—matching it to a skein of natural raffia. I mixed lemon yellow and yellow ochre—with just a touch of leaf green to give it a lovely fresh tone. But if you are buying paint specially, medium yellow added to white will be quite satisfactory—or you *could* even mix the medium yellow with plenty of water and use it alone, but you would get a warmer colour.

Using a 1-in.-wide household paint-brush, I sloshed the wet paint on to white crêpe paper, working from side-to-side in lines *along* the grain of the paper. It is essential to use a good quality crêpe, otherwise it will disintegrate. When the paper was soaking wet—and I was quite convinced it was utterly ruined—I left it hanging in a warm place to dry. To my surprise, the result was rather stiff, uneven, slightly crinkled—absolutely perfect sheets of home-grown maize!

I substituted stranded embroidery cotton for the hair "silk"—choosing a slightly darker shade than my paper. The rest was simple, as you can see from the few additional materials and easy directions below.

Materials

White crêpe paper
Poster paints (as above)
Natural raffia
Matching cotton
Stranded embroidery cotton
Plasticine (white or stone)
Pipe cleaners
Cotton wool
Black ink or felt pen
Fabric adhesive

19

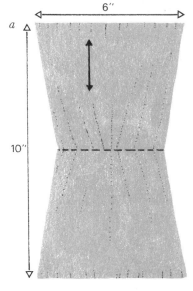

a

6″

10″

Method

Colour the crêpe paper as described above.

Cut a piece of crêpe 10 ins. deep by 6 ins. wide for the body (see diagram *a*: arrows indicate direction of grain). Gather this neatly across the centre with the finger-tips (as indicated by broken line) and tie tightly with cotton. Fold in half (diagram *b*).

Roll some plasticine into a ball the size of a large marble. Insert this between the folded paper, close under the tied centre, and smooth the paper round so that it leaves a flat area on one side for the face: tie tightly underneath (diagram *c*).

Cut a piece of crêpe for the arms 4 ins. deep by 6 ins. wide (grain running across—see diagram *d*). Cut a 3½-in. length of pipe cleaner and wrap a little cotton wool round the centre. Place near one edge of the paper (as in diagram *d*), and then roll the paper loosely round it, tying tightly with cotton ⅜ in. from each end: trim cut ends and tie a narrow strip of raffia round each wrist, over the cotton (diagram *e*). Place the arms between the body, close under the neck, and tie tightly underneath (diagram *f*).

Cut the skirt 6 ins. deep by 12 ins. wide (diagram *g*). Fold in half *across* the grain (broken line): then open out flat again. Thread a needle with double cotton and gather along the fold line: fold again, then draw up gathers as tightly as possible and secure. Fit round the waist, join ends at the back, and then drive the needle through the body and back again, catching front of skirt to waist as you do so. Trim lower edge if necessary, so that the figure stands steadily.

Cut the apron 6 ins. deep by 2 ins. wide. The broken lines on diagram *h* indicate folds: fold the lower 2 ins. up and then stick the edge of the top 1½ ins. over it. Turn over, slip a length of raffia through under the top fold, draw up slightly, and tie round waist.

Cut a 2-yd. length of embroidery cotton for the hair. Wind this evenly round a 2½-in.-deep piece of card. Tie the loops at each side, then slide gently off

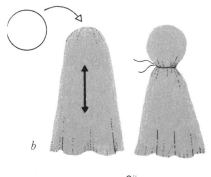

b

c

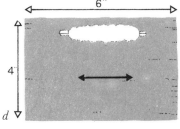

6″

4″

d

e

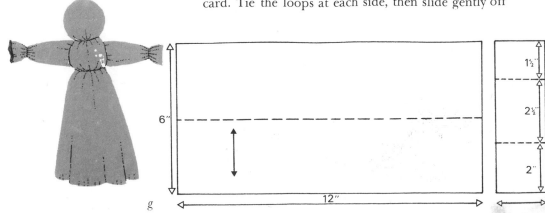

f

g

6″

12″

1½″

2½″

2″

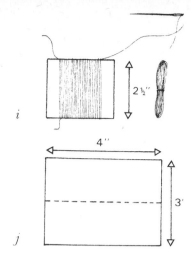

i

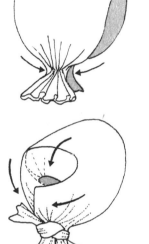

j

k

l

the card and tie the centre *loosely* with cotton (diagram *j*). Stick centre to top of head, then each side.

Cut the bonnet 3 ins. deep by 4 ins. wide (see diagram *j*) and fold in half along the grain to measure 1½ ins. by 4 ins. Place round head, folded edge to the front, and gather the ends in to the neck at sides and back: then fold back edge down and each side towards the centre, sticking one over the other as diagram *k*. Tie round neck with raffia.

Mark two dots for eyes with black ink or felt pen.

The old lady gathering kindling is made in exactly the same way, but she wears a headscarf instead of a bonnet. This is simply a 3-in. square of paper, folded diagonally: smear a little adhesive on the two front corners, twist them together, then pull the scarf gently over the head and stick at the back. Her bundle of sticks is attached to her back by a length of raffia looped round each side, crossing over her chest and tied under one arm. I inserted a length of pipe cleaner inside the upper half of the body to hold her bent position.

The little girl is made in just the same way as her mother, but the measurements are different:

Body 8 ins. deep by 10 ins. wide
Arms 4 ins. deep by 3½ ins. wide (3-in. pipe cleaner)
Skirt 4 ins. deep by 8 ins. wide
Apron 3 ins. deep by 1½ ins. wide (finished length 1¼ ins.)

Make a slightly smaller ball of plasticine for her head, and use less cotton wool inside the arms. Her hair is 4 yds. stranded cotton wound round a 5-in.-deep card: do not tie sides, but slide off very carefully and tie centre loosely. Stick to top of head, then sides, drawing round to the back, as illustrated.

To make the baby, cut the body paper 4 ins. deep by 2 ins. wide: gather and tie centre, insert a tiny ball of plasticine and tie underneath as before. Cut the bonnet 1 in. deep by 3 ins. wide and fold along grain to measure ½ in. by 1 in. Wrap over head and stick front corners. Tie several 1-in. lengths of stranded cotton together tightly at the centre, then fold in half, trim cut ends evenly and stick to head inside top of bonnet. Fold a 4-in. square of paper diagonally for the shawl. Wrap round the baby, crossing over at the front as diagram *e*: then fold each side back along broken lines and bind with raffia as illustrated. Mark eyes and fix in mother's arms.

Out of the orchard and into the kitchen

In the past—especially in country districts—the domestic life of the home centred round the kitchen and the kitchen garden. The kitchen was the most important room in the farmhouse or cottage, and the prudent housewife tended her herb garden and watched over the growing fruit and vegetables with a well-trained eye.

Today we tend to rely on the supermarket and the frozen-food cabinet for much of what used to be home-grown. But there's still plenty of imaginative material in your own kitchen—even if you didn't collect the eggs, pick the fruit or gather the vegetables yourself.

Here's an assortment of decorative articles for a variety of occasions—all with one thing in common: they're based on items out of the larder or store cupboard . . . despite the fact that the apples were imported and the eggs came in a plastic carton!

Country bonnet peaches

Smooth-skinned, juicy peaches, freshly ripened in the warm sun, are dressed up in romantic summer bonnets reminiscent of that nostalgic musical, "Oklahoma!". Make throwaway versions from paper and doilies, if they're just a fun table decoration for an adult party: but my miniature millinery is specially designed for little girls with fashion-conscious dolls! The fabrics and trimmings, of course, depend on the contents of your own piece bag: my materials are only for guidance.

Gingham bonnet

Materials

Scraps of gingham
altogether about 9 ins.
square)
Hat buckram or thin
card
$\frac{1}{4}$ yd. lace daisies or
similar trimming
6 ins. narrow braid
$\frac{1}{2}$ yd. narrow ribbon
Fabric adhesive

Method

On a piece of paper, draw a 5-in. diameter semi-circle and add 1 in. at the base, as diagram *a*. Cut this, and also a 2½-in. diameter circle, in buckram.

Stick gingham over one side of the buckram, trimming the fabric level with the buckram all round the curved edge, but allowing it to overlap about $\frac{3}{8}$ in.

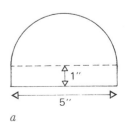

a

23

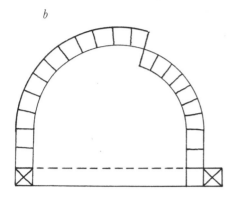

b

along the lower, straight, edge. Then stick gingham over the other side of the buckram, allowing it to overlap ⅜ in. all round. Snip the surplus fabric all round the curved edge into small tabs: turn over and stick to other side, as diagram *b* (broken line indicates edge of buckram): this is the inside of the brim.

Now snip the double fabric overlapping the straight edge into tabs, cutting away the corners marked X in the diagram. Stick these tabs round the edge of the buckram circle (see diagram *c*), and then cut the circle straight, between the sides of the brim, as indicated by the broken line.

Cut a 3-in. diameter circle of gingham, stick over the back of the bonnet, overlapping equally all round the curved edge: cut this surplus into tabs and stick round back edge of brim (diagram *d*). Trim surplus at each side, and stick remaining fabric up inside back.

Stick lace daisies all round inner edge of brim, and stick braid over tabs round back of brim. Cut ribbon in half and stitch at each side at angle indicated in diagram *d*, then trim with a lace daisy;

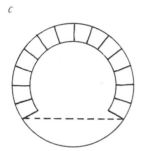

c

Lace trimmed bonnet

Method

Cut an 8-in.-diameter semi-circle of fabric.

Stitch lace to right side of fabric, all round curved edge of semi-circle, placing straight inner edge of lace ⅜ in. inside the raw edge of the fabric (see diagram *e*).

Materials

Scrap of flowered cotton
⅜ yd; 1-in.-wide lace
½ yd. narrow ribbon
Narrow round elastic

d

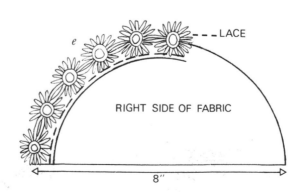

e

- - - LACE

RIGHT SIDE OF FABRIC

8″

Then turn under raw curved edge of fabric, level with stitching line of lace, and make a narrow hem all round.

Turn up straight lower edge of fabric and gather, drawing up to measure 4 ins. Thread elastic through hem round curved edge and draw up to fit your peach. Cut ribbon in half and stitch at each side, at the same angle as for the gingham bonnet.

Edwardian straw hat

Method

Use three strands of raffia—either cutting long lengths and joining in fresh pieces as necessary or, as I did, drawing from three separate skeins (two cream and one beige). Thread a tapestry or long darning needle with another length of raffia, then knot the end of this piece together with the ends of the three other pieces.

Twist the three strands together in a circle round the knot, and begin to oversew to hold in place, continuing round and round, catching each new circle to the previous one, as diagram *a*. Keeping the circle absolutely flat, continue in this way until it measures 3 ins. to $3\frac{1}{2}$ ins. in diameter, according to the size of your peach. Finish off neatly by cutting the three strands of raffia, one at a time.

Gather across the centre of the lace, draw up and stitch to centre of circle. Stitch a spray of tiny artificial or dried flowers over the gathered lace, heads towards the front, as illustrated. Then make the ribbon into a bow and stitch on top. Gather each end of the lace and draw up. Fit hat on peach and pin ends of lace underneath.

Cut $\frac{3}{4}$-in. squares of black crêpe paper for the eyes. Snip two-thirds (along grain) to form eyelashes, as diagram *b*: then curl slightly by drawing the "lashes" smoothly between the ball of your thumb and the blade of a knife or scissors. Stick to the peach.

Make the hair from a strip of brown tissue paper, gathered and tied at the centre, then draped round the peach under the hat, as illustrated.

Materials

Natural or coloured raffia
9–10 ins. $2\frac{1}{2}$-in.-wide lace, chiffon or net
6 ins. $1\frac{1}{2}$-in.-wide velvet ribbon
Tiny flowers

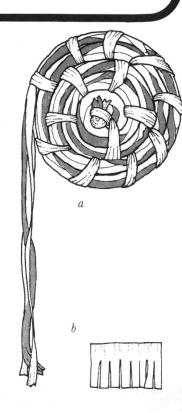

a

b

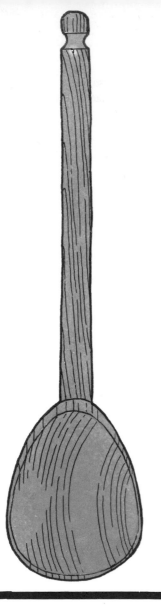

Wooden spoon wall decorations

I am fascinated by wooden spoons: they're such solid, comfortable, *homely* objects. . . . Even in this modern machine age, nothing has been invented to replace the friendly wooden spoon, which was as basic an item in grandmother's kitchen as it was in her grandmother's before her.

That natural, smoothly turned wood seemed worthy of better things than only the mixing bowl, and I thought of the highly valued wooden spoons which young Welsh lovers used to carve and paint for their sweethearts—to be proudly displayed on the wall in days gone by.

Here is my suggestion for an attractive spoon wall hanging: I have made three variations as visual examples—you can see them in the colour picture on page 18.

Materials

A wooden spoon (those illustrated are 12 ins., 10 ins. and 8 ins. long)
Dried flowers, grasses, barley, oats, etc.
Ribbon, lace, etc., to trim
Clear adhesive tape
Thread to hang

Method

Bunch together flower-heads, grasses, barley, etc. to fill bowl of spoon, cutting the stalks about 2 ins. long. Fit in place, then tape stalks securely to base of handle to hold in position.

Bunch together more of the dried materials, cut stalks as before, and tape further up the handle to cover previous tape. Continue in this way, turning the final bunch in the other direction if you like (see largest spoon).

Make a small bow of toning ribbon, raffia, lace, etc., and stitch in position over final tape.

Hang by a loop of thread suspended from the top of the handle.

"*Summer* collage"

using dried vegetables and string

Materials

Butter beans
Split yellow peas
Split green peas
Pearl barley
Spaghetti
String
Dishcloth knitting yarn
A piece of heavy card
(mine is 22 ins. by 12
ins.)
Dark brown woven
linen-type fabric, 1 in.
larger all round than
the card
Strong adhesive tape
Clear all-purpose
adhesive
Adhesive tabs or rings to
hang

I raided the store cupboard for dried pulse vegetables and pasta—the string box providing the stalks, with dishcloth cotton edging the leaves. The result was a highly stylised flower collage. Here's my recipe—but don't hesitate to let your own store cupboard dictate *your* composition. For instance, I sternly resisted buying some spaghetti spirals, rings and shells especially for the purpose—but *wouldn't* they be fun!

Method

Cover the card with fabric, allowing the excess to overlap equally all round: turn over each side and tape raw edges neatly to the back, trimming and turning in the corners neatly.

Very roughly work out your design before you begin, taking into consideration the shape of your picture background, and the materials you are using.

I arranged six butter beans in a 2-in.-diameter circle just above the centre of my vertical panel, sticking them in position when I was satisfied, and filling the centre in with split green peas—always using plenty of adhesive. Then I cut a petal shape in paper, and drew round it six times, using a white crayon, to form my flower. I encircled the butter beans, picked out the edge of the petals and made a line up the centre of each, with split yellow peas. Using lots of adhesive, I then filled in each petal by sprinkling pearl barley liberally over it and patting it down—shaking off the excess afterwards.

The upper flower is five butter beans, a green pea and an edging of yellow peas, forming a 2½-in.-diameter flower—with strips of spaghetti between the petals.

The lower flower is made up of a circle of nine butter beans around a green pea centre, making a 2¾-in.-diameter flower.

I designed my leaf shape on paper, then cut it out and arranged it in positions to balance the flowers —then drew round it as before, drawing in linking stalks at the same time. These I picked out in heavy parcel string (or you could use piping cord), with a thinner string for the two small flowers. I stuck dishcloth yarn over the leaf outlines, then filled them in with bright green peas.

Fix tabs or rings at the back to hang.

Dainty eggs for Easter

Hens' eggs can be decorated in a variety of ways for truly traditional Easter eggs. I have shown four ideas which are rather more delicate than the usual brightly painted and coloured versions.

Hard-boil the eggs, if you don't want to keep them permanently. Otherwise blow them. Using a darning needle, make a small hole at the pointed end of the egg and a slightly larger one at the round end: stir the yolk up inside with the needle. Holding the egg over a bowl, blow through the pointed end, until the shell is completely empty. Wash thoroughly and leave standing upright to dry.

Using clear all-purpose adhesive, stick the decoration all over the eggshell. I used grass seed-heads for one; pink, blue and white lace flowers for another; motifs cut from a silver paper doily for the third; and for the last, pastel-coloured icing motifs sold for cake decorating.

Hallowe'en apple witches

Spell-binding apples for a Hallowe'en party: these wicked witches are quick to make, but so amusing they make a striking table decoration (especially guarding the punch-bowl!).

Materials

Apples
Black cartridge paper
Black crêpe paper
Thin card
Red paper
Coloured plasticine
Garden raffia
Thin garden canes
Small flower-pots
Fabric adhesive

Method

Cut an 8-in.-radius quarter-circle of black cartridge paper for the body, cutting away a 2-in.-radius section at the corner (see diagram *a*). Curve round into a cone and stick the straight edges.

Cut a 16-in.-diameter semi-circle of black crêpe paper for the cloak, cutting away a 4-in.-diameter semi-circle in the centre (see diagram *b*—arrows indicate grain). Bring the two straight edges down to meet at the centre (diagram *c*): do not crease folds. Stick round top edge. With this side inside the cloak, stick top edge round top of cone (join in cone at the back).

Cut a 4-in.-radius quarter-circle of black cartridge paper for the hat, cutting away a ¼-in.-radius section

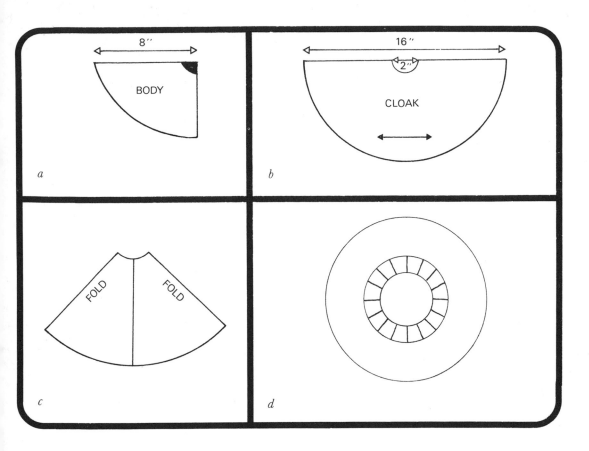

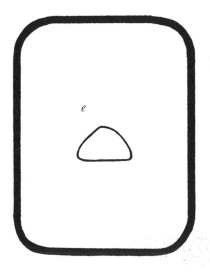

at the corner. Curve round into a cone and stick straight edges. Cut a 4-in.-diameter circle of thin card, with a $2\frac{1}{4}$-in.-diameter circle in the centre, for the brim. Cover one side with black paper and cut edges level with card. Cover the other side with black paper: cut outer edge level, but cut away only a 1-in.-diameter circle in the centre. Cut remaining black paper at centre into tabs (diagram d), bend up and stick inside lower edge of the hat.

Bunch together some 12-in. lengths of raffia and tie at the centre. Push cane down centre of body cone and anchor end in an up-turned flower-pot inside: cut cane $1\frac{1}{2}$ ins. above cone and push the apple down on to it. Fix raffia on top for hair, with the hat on top of that.

Make eyes as directed for bonnet apples. Model nose in plasticine. Trace and cut the mouth (diagram e) in red paper. Stick into position as illustrated, fixing the nose on the head of a pin.

Flowers with a future

✂ Bear in mind

Glixia are tiny, star-like flowers which add immeasurably to so many everlasting decorations that they are well worth buying. And I do mean *buying*. Because it is their vibrant colours which make them so striking, and these are achieved by dyeing the dried heads. So even if you are able to grow the flowers yourself, or buy natural-coloured ones, it simply isn't worth the additional expense and trouble of buying a selection of dyes to colour your own. On the other hand, straw-daisies are much cheaper, and more fun to grow—appearing in a rich assortment of golden-yellows and pinky-mauves.

But a small bunch of glixia supplies far more heads than you expect, and if you buy the bunches over a period of time, you will soon have a good colour range.

3 *Preserving flowers and foliage*

Many people don't realise how many of the plants they grow in their own gardens provide ideal material for drying. I have already mentioned honesty and straw-daisies—which virtually dry themselves when grown in a sunny position—but delphiniums, hydrangeas and zinnias are all good for drying, along with the better-known statice, achillea, Chinese lanterns, grasses and gourds. Then, of course, you can preserve leaves, ferns and showy seed-heads like old man's beard. So there's no reason to be short of flowers or foliage even at the most barren time of the year. And there is the added advantage that dried and other "everlasting" material doesn't wilt and die like a fresh arrangement—so your flowers really do have a future.

Here is a count-down of some of the more common flowers and foliage which are really simple to dry or preserve. But don't forget that almost *any* flower can be preserved—it's just a matter of the method used. Marigolds, for instance, can be dried in borax, but I haven't listed them here, as it is a rather involved procedure. However, if you are keen, find a book which deals specifically with the subject of preserving flowers and foliage for decoration: some of the methods are fascinating, and most ingenious.

Achillea is a flat-headed plant (usually yellow) with a strong scent and fern-like leaves: it looks a little like cow parsley. The head is composed of a mass of tiny flowers, and these should be fully open before it is gathered. Then hang upside-down in a dry place, away from strong sunlight.

Acroclinium: These open-petalled daisies have the advantage of stems which dry with the flower. Gather them when the flowers are fully open, and dry as for achillea.

Chinese lanterns: Wait until the lowest lanterns on each stem turn orange: then pick them, remove the leaves, and hang up to dry as for achillea—when the remaining lanterns will also turn colour.

Clary: When all the pink, leaf-like petals at the top of the stem are fully open, pick the stems and hang up to dry as for achillea.

Delphiniums: If you want to dry whole spikes, gather them when the lowest flower opens—or pick the newly-opened flowers and the bud stems. Hang them, separately, upside-down in a warm room away from the sun—or, better still, in a warm airing cupboard. Wait until the flowers are so dry they are almost like tissue paper.

Honesty: Allow the seed-heads to form and the stems to become dry before picking: then remove the leaves and hang in a warm, airy room. When thoroughly dry, rub away the outer, protective covering and the seed, leaving just the silver-white papery circles.

Hydrangeas: There is a tiny flower in the centre of each flower making up the whole head. It's not until these have faded, and the outer petals become absolutely dry, that the head is ready to be picked. Hang upside-down to dry as for delphiniums.

Statice: Wait until these colourful flowers are fully open and matured, then gather them on a dry day and hang upside-down away from the sun, as for achillea. Big bunches of fresh statice are often inexpensive to buy, but should be divided into smaller bunches before hanging up to dry as above.

Straw-daisies (helichrysums): If you pick the flowers before they are quite fully open, you will be able to retain the lovely rich colours of these hardy daisies. Either bunch them and hang upside-down to dry, as for achillea—or else cut off the heads and lay them on a rack in a dry place away from the sun. If you want to use them as stems, leave about an inch of stalk behind the head and insert a florist's wire immediately.

Zinnias: The light colours—yellow, cream and white—will be the most satisfactory. Gather when all the petals are fully open, and dry them in a warm airing cupboard.

Grasses, corn, barley, wheat, oats, etc.: These must be cut when they are young and not yet fully ripe, otherwise the seed-heads will drop. Tie into bunches and hang upside-down in a warm place, away from strong sun, to dry.

Beech, oak, laurel, camellia leaves, etc.: Add one part glycerine to two parts boiling water. Allow the stems to stand to a depth of two inches in this solution for two to three weeks, until the leaves change colour and become glossy and slightly polished looking.

Ferns: Stand them in a glycerine solution, as for leaves, for two or three days, then press between sheets of blotting paper under a weight.

Old man's beard: Watch for the seed-heads to form, but pick before they become fluffy. Then stand in glycerine solution as for leaves until the heads become fluffy.

Now try some imaginative ways of using your dried and everlasting material—whether it is all home-grown or bought ready-preserved.

Statice pomander ball

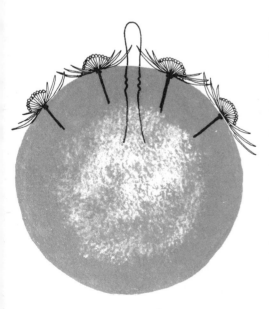

In Tudor times every lady of quality always took the precaution of wearing a pomander suspended from her waist when she ventured out among the common people. This often bejewelled and beautifully worked ornament of precious metal was nevertheless not just an ostentatious vanity: it was a sensible means of avoiding the many unpleasant smells which pervaded the streets—and, they believed, a protection against plague or other infection. The hollow ball was either made in an open-work design, or else punctured all over with small holes, and the inside was filled with fragrant perfumes, herbs and spices.

In a traditional Lenten custom which is still observed every year, the British monarch distributes "Maundy money" to old people in London's parish of Westminster—and still carries a posy, or nosegay, of flowers!

Another form of pomander ball is a later innovation enjoying a revival today. Simply stud the whole surface of an orange closely with cloves, and when it is dry, hang it in your wardrobe to discourage moths.

I have combined these mementoes of earlier centuries in a dried flower pomander ball to hang beside a window, on a bedroom wall, or from the mirror of a dainty dressing table. And I cannot imagine a prettier alternative to the usual posy of fresh flowers carried by a bridesmaid—especially as it is something she can keep afterwards to remind her of the important part she played in the great day.

The ball is simplicity itself to make, needing only the styrofoam base, dried flower-heads—and patience. But stabbing the stalks home and watching the massed petals gradually spread over the surface of the ball is such a fascinating and relaxing occupation that one doesn't have time to become bored.

Almost any small flower can be substituted, and styrofoam balls can be obtained in at least three sizes : they are sold by florists and the artificial flower and decorations departments of large stores.

Materials

Statice and/or similar
dried flower-heads
A 3½-in.-diameter
styrofoam ball
A heavy (approximately
2½-in.) metal hair pin
½ yd. ribbon to hang

Method

Break or cut the flower-heads to leave $\frac{1}{4}$–$\frac{1}{2}$ in. of stalk, then push the dry stalk into the styrofoam until the base of the petals is against the surface. If you have difficulty pushing them in, or the stalks break, make a small hole first with the point of a small pair of scissors or a darning needle.

Continue in this way, massing the heads closely together, until the ball is completely covered. For the prettiest results, choose not more than three colours, and either mix them to give an all-over mottled effect, or make a pattern, as I have done on the two examples illustrated.

Towards the end, push the hair pin into the ball, leaving about $\frac{1}{2}$ in. protruding: thread ribbon (or ribbons, as in the pink and blue ball) through to hang, then push the pin down until it is hidden by the petals.

Tiny sprigs of other dried foliage may be pushed in between the petals to extend beyond them and given an even more delicate appearance: I have done this on the violet and yellow ball.

A boxful of flowers

If you dry your own straw-daisies, you will find that the stalks become very brittle, and will need to be replaced by wires if you plan to use them as stems. However, if you have a collection of heads, here is a charming way to display them on their own.

The little box is simply made of thick card covered with pieces cut from an inexpensive bamboo or straw table mat (bamboo mats often have a design painted on the right side: don't worry—just use the plain underside). Then all you have to do is fill the inside with flower-heads, allowing some to peep over the front edge, so that the lid is slightly raised when resting on the petals.

Materials

A bamboo or straw table mat (about 12 ins. by 18 ins.)
Thick card
Dried flower-heads
Toning face tissue
Strong adhesive tape
Clear all-purpose adhesive

Method

Cut a piece of card to the measurements and shape shown in diagram *a*: it is important to measure and cut accurately, checking right angles with a set square. Partially cut or score the broken lines, then turn card over and score on the reverse side. Also cut a piece of card $3\frac{1}{2}$ ins. by $6\frac{1}{2}$ ins., for the lid.

Bend up the scored sections to form the sides of the box: fix each corner neatly with tape (on the outside).

Now place the box on one long side and lay the lid flat beside it, touching the top edge of the box (edge of lid and top edge of box are indicated by the broken line in diagram *b*). Tape this join, to form a hinge inside the box.

Measure and cut a length of table mat, slightly wider than the lid, and long enough to reach from the hinged back of the lid inside the box, over the top of the lid, down the back of the box and underneath, ending at the front edge of the base—plus a little extra (about 13–14 ins. in all): make sure the bamboo or straw runs across the lid, so that it folds round the corners, and cut so that the strands running in the reverse direction, which hold the mat together, fall at an equal distance from each side (see illustration).

Stick the strip of mat round the lid and box as described above: remove surplus straws at the end, and stick remaining threads neatly to the card.

Cut a long strip of mat the same depth as the box and long enough (plus a little) to cover both sides and the front, the straws running down. Stick round the box, finishing off each back edge as before.

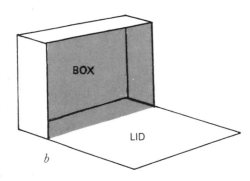

BOX

LID

b

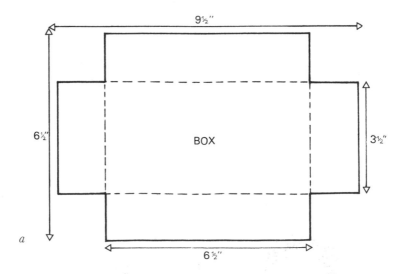

a

9½″

6½″

3½″

BOX

6½″

To arrange the straw-daisies as illustrated, place a face tissue (pink or yellow, according to your colour-scheme) flat on the table. Stick the flower-heads closely together to cover the tissue to within about an inch of the edge all round. Then trim away excess tissue just below the petals of the outer flowers.

When dry, fit the flower-covered tissue inside the box, overlapping the front edge, as illustrated.

Evergreen candle branch

All evergreens are a joy, but I particularly love ivy. I *know* it clings to all sorts of things it shouldn't cling to, and eats away bricks, and strangles weaker plants. . . . I know all its disadvantages, and just how severely it needs to be kept in check. But I still love it! Perhaps because I hate the starkness of winter so much—when the ivy is one of the few patches of green against the dark brown earth and bare trees. Its prettily-shaped, polished leaves mass so closely together, bravely defying the elements and reminding one of holly and mistletoe and Christmas.

But even if *you* haven't my special feelings for ivy, you can't deny its versatility for decoration. We have three clumps growing in the garden—all spreading just as rapidly as I snip bits off them. One is a glossy dark green, the second a delicate cream and the other variegated. Our plants are only in the garden because they became a nuisance over-growing their pots indoors. So if you have only a window box or sill, your ivy will flourish just as happily there (and you'll enjoy it more, too).

I have designed this particular decoration to incorporate ever*green* as well as everlasting materials. I chose ivy as my theme—but holly, laurel leaves, spruce—or even preserved brown oak or beech leaves, would be an equally suitable alternative. Vary the size, shape and composition of your "branch" as much as you please: this one is intended to stand isolated on a polished table-top for a formal occasion. But a single candle set on a much smaller piece of bark, with just a few flowers and leaves, would make a charming table centre for a small dinner party . . . with three or four down the middle of a

Materials

Cork bark to required size (obtainable from florists)
Dried flower-heads (I used statics)
Ivy or other evergreen
Candles (mine are 8 ins. long)
Wax crayons, frosting, etc. (optional)
Dark green plasticine
Fine wire or cotton
Pins
All-purpose adhesive (optional)

long table for a larger gathering. Shiny holly with plenty of berries, and scarlet candles frosted with aerosol "snow", would make a cheerful adaptation for Christmas.

The "home-crafted" candles in my example are a quick and easy—utterly shameless—cheat! I buy cheap candles, then decorate the surface with children's wax crayons, as described in Chapter 5.

Method

Break your bark to the size and shape you require. Make sure it stands firmly by fixing wedges of plasticine underneath.

If using wax crayons to decorate your candles, do this now (see Chapter 5), or prepare them with an alternative choice of decoration—but it is wiser to leave aerosol frosting until the arrangement is complete.

Roll a lump of plasticine about the size of a table tennis ball, then press the base of a candle into it. Make sure the candle is firmly embedded—then press it down very firmly into position on the bark "branch". Either squeeze a blob of adhesive on to the spot before pressing the plasticine down, or secure with pins (or do both). Make sure the candle is standing straight and is still firmly gripped by the plasticine. Repeat with remaining candle or candles.

Wire or tie together small bunches of dried flower-heads, then pin them at appropriate spots into crevices in the bark.

Finally, trail sprigs of ivy or other evergreen round the base of the candles and over the branch as illustrated, pressing the stalks down into the plasticine to hold them securely in place.

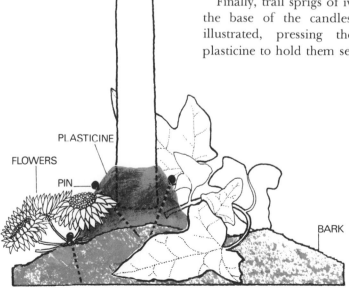

FLOWERS
PLASTICINE
PIN
BARK

Picture it in flowers

4

Bear in mind

"Collage" comes from the french *coller*: to paste or glue. and when using dried flowers and foliage, the adhesive is all-important: it is essential to use the correct type, and to apply it carefully but reasonably generously. I use a clear all-purpose adhesive for almost everything. This is stronger than fabric adhesive, and shows less. For very fine pieces, double-sided tape can be very useful.

As a rule, I use wallpaper paste to stick my backgrounds smoothly. Mitre the corners if there is an overlap, turn over to the wrong side and neaten the raw edges at the back with strips of adhesive tape.

Don't be afraid to buy dyed flowers and foliage: they are often so striking that one, or two contrasting varieties combined with natural pieces of your own, will *make* a picture.

Collage pictures are one of the most attractive and creatively rewarding things you can make with dried flowers and foliage—and often you need no more than a few stalks for the most effective results.

But don't jump to the conclusion that, if you're not artistic, you might as well skip this chapter. First, you don't need to have creative talent at all to copy the pictures illustrated on pages 38 and 39—just follow the step-by-step directions (even if you substitute different flowers, the principle is the same). Secondly, it is the actual method that is important— knowing *how* to do it: once you know that, you'll find that nature, in her own inimitable way, does much of the work for you. A few stalks, arranged and re-arranged, gradually fall into their happiest positions in relation to each other and their setting, and you will find your picture has created itself . . . just as plants growing informally in a cottage garden always mass to form a perfectly natural display, seeking out the sun and turning their colourful blooms towards its warmth.

Use your own preserved materials—or choose brilliantly contrasting shades from the irresistible dyed bunches sold commercially: I do both, as you can see. Incidentally, I find tremendous inspiration for backgrounds in a packet of assorted sheets of children's coloured construction paper: this gives you a wide selection of light and dark colours ideal for flower pictures, and is cheaper than buying separate sheets of art paper.

After the harvest

A few stalks of bleached grain and grasses on a dark linen ground, suggesting the edge of the harvest field, demonstrate perfectly how very simple natural collage can be. So I will use this example to explain the basic method. Substitute your own materials, as required.

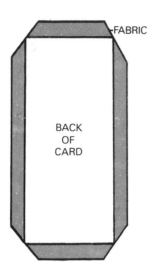

FABRIC

BACK
OF
CARD

Method

Trim the card to size and then cover one side thickly with wallpaper paste. Press this side down firmly on to the wrong side of the fabric, so that it overlaps equally all round. Make sure the fabric is stretched absolutely smoothly over the surface of the card, then mitre the corners (cut away a triangle as diagram) and fold the excess neatly over the sides and stick to the back of the card. Tape the raw edge of the fabric to the card all round.

Arrange your grain and grass-heads on the fabric surface, cutting the stalks to length as you decide on the position of each piece: always bear in mind the way they would look growing naturally in the fields—perhaps swaying slightly in the wind. (Having made that statement, I rather contradicted it by trimming the "whiskers" off my barley because they were so long they fell off the edge of the picture!) You will notice that all my stems radiate from one corner, which I have finished with a single straw-daisy: this is a useful trick to remember when you want to hide the spot where your stalks converge.

Having decided on your arrangement, try to move the individual pieces as little as possible as you stick each one into place separately, using clear adhesive. However, it is wise to mark the position of each with pins, so that it won't matter if the parts are disarranged.

Begin at one side, sticking the longest piece into place. Do this by coating the back with a trail of clear adhesive and then pressing it firmly into position. Follow with the piece next to it, and continue round to finish at the other side with the shortest stalks, completing with a flower over the cut ends as illustrated.

Fix tabs or rings at the back to hang.

Materials

Grain, grass-heads and flowers, as shown
A piece of heavy card 14 ins. by 6 ins.
Coarsely woven fabric 1 in. larger all round (16 ins. by 8 ins.)
Wallpaper paste
Clear all-purpose adhesive
Strong adhesive tape
$\frac{1}{2}$-in. steel pins (optional)
Adhesive tabs or rings to hang

Straw-daisy circuit

A few dried flowers make an enchanting wall decoration in which the most important factor is effective colour-scheming. I laid my golden-brown straw-daisies on an olive green ground and then echoed the colour of the flowers again in the velvet mount. Equally dramatic are pinky-mauve straw-daisies on a cream ground with a purple velvet mount.

I interspersed my straw-daisies with deep cream glixia and paler statice heads—but any combination of flowers, or flowers and foliage, could be substituted for the three I have used for my circlet.

Method

Cut a 6-in. square of card for the background, and an 8-in. square for the mount.

Paste coloured paper over the background as described for the previous picture, omitting the tape. Cover the mount with velvet in the same way, using all-purpose adhesive and finishing the back with tape over the raw edges of the velvet.

Find the centre of the background square (by marking the spot where diagonals from corner to corner cross) and draw a $4\frac{1}{2}$-in.-diameter circle. Place your straw-daisies—or alternative main flower—in position over the marked line.

Wire, or bind together with cotton, tiny bunches of glixia and statice heads, as illustrated, making them large enough to fill the spaces between the daisies.

When the circle is complete, stick each piece into place separately with clear adhesive, working round the circle so that the daisy petals cover the stalks of the miniature bunches. Use tiny pins, the heads carefully hidden beneath the petals, to hold both the daisies and the bunches in place securely.

To complete, stick the background on to the velvet mount and fix tabs or rings at the back to hang.

Materials

6 straw-
daisies
Glixia   } or alternatives
Statice
Heavy card (6 ins. square
and 8 ins. square)
Coloured paper for
background (8 ins.
square)
Velvet for mount (10 ins.
square)
Fine wire or cotton
Wallpaper paste
Clear all-purpose
adhesive
Strong adhesive tape
$\frac{1}{2}$-in. steel pins.
Adhesive tabs or rings to
hang

October blaze

This small wall plaque in scarlet and brown illustrates just how little you need to compose an eye-catching collage. I have cheated just a little by curving the heavier grass round to follow the shape of the circle—but no more than it might bend in the wind.

Again, substitute your own materials and colour scheme as you wish: just be sure you are satisfied with your arrangement before you begin to stick the pieces into place.

45

Materials

Heavy brown grass-heads
Fluffy brown grass heads
Red grass-heads or alternatives
Red glixia
heavy card
Pale pink coloured paper to cover
½ yd. ½-in.-wide string-coloured woven braid
Wallpaper paste
Clear all-purpose adhesive
Adhesive tab or ring to hang

Method

Paste the coloured paper smoothly over the circle of card and trim the edges level.

Work out the composition of the picture as before, then stick the largest grass-head into position with clear adhesive, curving it round to follow the shape of the circle and holding it in place until it is securely stuck. Follow with the next grass-head, sticking it in the same way, continuing with the remaining heads as illustrated—the stalks meeting at the same point (as in the first picture).

Finally stick glixia heads in a group over the converging stalks, following the illustration.

Stick braid round the outer edge of the circle, and fix a tab or ring at the back to hang.

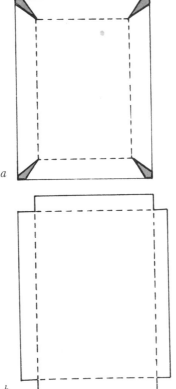

Springtime

I chose the fresh green and yellow of early spring for this more formal arrangement set in a deep velvet frame. The principle is just the same, though: compose your picture first, then stick the pieces down individually. And the rather spectacular frame is perfectly simple when you know how—it's just a matter of careful measuring and accurate cutting with a sharp knife. Scheme your velvet border to pick up one of the colours in your picture.

Method

Cut a piece of card 9½ ins. by 6½ ins. for the background and cover with white or coloured paper, 1 in. larger all round, pasting it smoothly over the surface and sticking the excess to the back of the card as described for the first picture (omitting tape).

46

Materials

Dyed green feathery
grass
Dyed green and yellow
oats
Heavy brown grass-
heads
Feathery brown grass
Small flowers in brown
and yellow (glixia,
etc.)
or alternatives
Stiff white card
White (or coloured)
paper for background
(11½ ins. by 8½ ins.)
1½ yds. 1½-in.-wide velvet
ribbon
1½ yds. lacy gilt braid
Fine wire or cotton
Wallpaper paste
Clear all-purpose
adhesive
Adhesive tape
½-in. steel pins (optional)
Double-sided tape
(optional)
Adhesive tabs or rings
to hang

Arrange your dried flowers and foliage on the back-ground, as before, building up from the back of the arrangement. I used a fluffy green grass to set off the brown and yellow pieces, fanning it out so that it formed the shape of the arrangement—with a few green oats at each side. The best way to stick this into place is to spread a coat of clear adhesive over this area of background and then press the grass lightly against it: alternatively, use double-sided tape.

The yellow oats and brown grasses followed, stuck in the usual way, then the glixia (bound into bunches) and the circle of small yellow flower-heads.

To make the frame, cut a piece of card 1½ ins. larger all round (12¼ ins. by 9¼ ins.). Mark the area of the picture in the centre (broken line in diagram a), then mark the outer edge of each side ½ in. from the corners: this must be very accurate. Now cut out a V-shaped piece at each corner, between the marked points and the corners of the inner rectangle (see diagram). Score the broken lines and bend the sides gently upwards. Stick a length of velvet ribbon neatly along each side, allowing it to overlap slightly at each end.

Cut another piece of card, 13¼ ins. by 10¼ ins., for the back of the frame. Measure a 1-in. border all round (broken line in diagram b), cut away the corners and score the broken line. Bend the sides up to form a box and tape the corners neatly.

Coat the back of the velvet-bordered mount with adhesive and press it down firmly into the "box", making sure the cut ends of the velvet are neatly tucked away behind. When securely fixed, stick the picture itself into place in the centre of the velvet mount.

Stick gilt braid round the edge of the "box", slightly overlapping the velvet as illustrated.

Fix tabs or rings at the back to hang.

Meadowsweet

Nostalgic Victoriana in pinks and mauves. I designed this oval picture for a bedroom, using cream linen for the background and gilt braid for the frame.

Once you know the secret of drawing a perfect oval, it isn't nearly as complicated as it looks. I give directions for an oval the same size as mine (12 ins. by 9 ins.)—but you can see how it adapts to any size you wish.

I used a small selection of the shades I wanted from a pack of assorted dried materials—plus my own home-grown straw-daisies. Choose flowers and foliage for your picture dyed to match your own personal colour-scheme.

Materials

Assorted dyed and
natural flowers and
foliage as preferred
Heavy card
Fabric or coloured
paper to cover
1 yd. gilt braid
Fine wire or cotton
Wallpaper paste
Clear all-purpose
adhesive
½-in. steel pins (optional)
Double-sided tape
(optional)
Adhesive tabs or rings to
hang

Method

Draw your oval on heavy card, following the diagram. First draw a 12-in.-long vertical line, A–B. Mark the centre (C) and then quarters (D and D). With the point of your compasses at D and radius 3 ins., draw a circle above and below C.

Now with centre C, draw a 4-in.-long horizontal line at right angles to A–B (E–F). With the point of your compasses at E, draw the arc G–G. And with the compasses point at F, draw the arc H–H. Cut out carefully with a sharp knife.

Paste linen smoothly over the surface of the card, overlapping 1 in. all round. Snip this surplus into small tabs and stick neatly over to the back of the card.

Arrange and stick the various pieces into position as previously described, using clear adhesive, double-sided tape and pins, as required.

Stick gilt braid round the outer edge to frame, and fix tabs or rings at the back to hang.

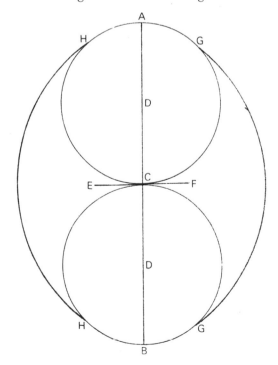

5

Lighting-up time

Five lamps and matching shades —and decorated candles and stands

Obviously you will be planning *your* lamps and shades for particular spots in your own home —and will have a very definite idea of the size you want your lamp or shade to be. I have given the measurements of *my* lamps and shades in detail merely as an indication, so that you can base your calculations on them.

You can get a good impression of proportions by sketching out the plans for your own lamp and shade on squared paper.

When decorating the candles, I have always used—as you will see— a flame to melt the wax. But if you want to avoid a slightly sooty effect when using clear, bright yellows and similar light colours, you can dip the wax crayon in boiling water instead of melting it in the flame. You *can* merge the colours to complete the candle in this way, too—but it is rather tricky to do, and tends to wash the coloured wax off the surface of the candle.

As the year draws towards its close, the days grow shorter and the sun sets a little earlier—so that the curtains are drawn cosily against the chill, dark evening, and lamps take the place of daylight, creating a warm air of comfort and well-being. This is the time for candles, too—casting a romantically soft glow and making intriguing shadows as their flames dance and flicker in the slightest draught.

I like a number of small table lamps, placed at convenient spots and set at different heights, around the room. And I love to see decorative candles gracing a mantelpiece or dining table, or just illuminating a dark corner. I am delighted that candles are enjoying such a popular revival, and are no longer reserved solely for the Christmas festivities: one should take advantage of their elegance and charm at every possible opportunity throughout the year!

Lamp bases can be an expensive item to buy—yet it is ridiculously easy to make your own from all manner of empty containers. Needless to say, there's nothing worse that a lamp that *looks* like an empty cocoa tin. But it *is* possible to make really smart bases—especially if you choose a good shape and key the colour to its future setting . . . and then team it with a toning shade. The secret is that it looks planned. As for shades, they are so quick and simple to make if you take advantage of modern materials, that only basic directions are necessary.

I have continued my "country" theme with this collection of lamps and shades—aiming at interesting textures, natural-looking materials and subtle colours.

Unusual candles can be very costly, too—particularly hand-made ones—so that one hesitates to light them except for important occasions. Which is a pity. But I have devised a technique for giving the cheapest household candles a very individual, home-crafted appearance—so that you can afford to burn them just for the enjoyment of making some more!

The lamps

Beige and brown textured base

I used a 4-ounce instant coffee jar for this one, 6 ins. high by 3 ins. in diameter—but any type of container with fairly straight sides would be suitable. And I used a "bubbly" textured knitting yarn: but again, substitute your own choice of yarn or wool—just remember that the more texture it has, the more effective the finish.

Method

Make sure the container is clean, then paste torn pieces of newspaper (no bigger than 1-inch square) evenly to cover the outside, the edges slightly overlapping: then paste another layer of newspaper over the first, then another, until the sides are completely covered with a thick layer of papier mâché. Repeat with several layers of tissue paper (use poor quality for the best results!) until no newsprint shows through. If the surface isn't absolutely smooth, so much the better. Leave in a warm place until thoroughly dried out.

When dry, paint thickly with poster colour and, when this is dry, begin to wind the yarn evenly round and round the container, criss-crossing the strands, until the surface is covered as illustrated. If you have difficulty on slopes, brush paste over the painted surface.

When you are satisfied with the finished appearance, brush paste very thickly indeed over the entire surface, until the yarn is completely saturated. Leave to dry.

If necessary, fill with rice, salt, sand, etc., to add weight. Then fit lamp adapter as instructions.

Materials

Empty container
Textured yarn or wool
Newspaper
Tissue paper
Poster paint (in a darker shade than yarn)
Wallpaper paste
A suitable lamp adapter

Moss green raffia base

This one is a small tomato ketchup bottle, 8 ins. high by $2\frac{1}{4}$ ins. diameter. But the method is the same, whatever you use.

Method

First cover the outside of the container with a layer of papier mâché, using first newspaper and then tissue paper, as instructed for the previous lamp. But do not allow to dry: instead, coat thickly with more paste.

Then, beginning at the top, wind raffia evenly round and round, *making sure the raffia is thoroughly wet with paste*, and *pulling it taut* so that it grips the bottle and does not stretch and slip. Continue until the

---

Materials

Empty container
Dull raffia
Newspaper
Tissue paper
Wallpaper paste
A suitable lamp adapter

Brown and bleached grass-heads base

container is completely covered, as illustrated. Coat with paste and leave to dry.

Weight, if necessary, as previous lamp, and fit adapter as instructions.

You need an attractive, straight-sided clear glass jar for this one: I used an old-fashioned apothecary jar, 5 ins. high by 2½ ins. diameter. These storage jars come in a variety of sizes, and are ideal for this purpose.

Materials

Apothecary, or similar clear glass jar
Brown grass-heads
Bleached grass-heads
Dyed green oats
(optional)
or alternatives

Method

Make sure the jar is absolutely clean and polished, inside and out.

Measure the height of the wide part of the jar, below the neck, and the circumference. Cut a piece of clear acetate or pvc this size, then roll it up and place it inside the jar so that it opens up: take it out and, if necessary, trim the height so that it will fit snugly against the sides of the jar.

Stick grass-heads side-by-side to cover the acetate or pvc (as for collage pictures), adding a few coloured oats near the lower edge if liked. When dry, roll the acetate round very carefully, grass-heads outside, and lower gently into the jar so that the roll opens out again inside and the grass is held between the acetate or pvc and the sides of the jar.

Fill the base with a layer of small stones, about ½ in. deep, and then fit lamp adapter as instructions.

Golden corn glass base

This attractive golden-brown glass jar held another brand of instant coffee—2-ounce size, height 4½ ins., diameter 2½ ins. I made it into a lamp base in exactly the same way as the apothecary jar—but alternated bleached grass-heads with ears of barley (their whiskers suitably trimmed!)

Green linen base

For an absolutely straight, cylindrical base, I used a sturdy lampshade frame 6½ ins. high by 4 ins. diameter. The "bonded" parchment is sold for making lampshades: it is specially treated on one side so that fabric adheres to it when ironed on. Use a fairly hot iron (test an odd piece first) and a damp cloth.

Materials

Cylindrical lampshade
frame
Linen to cover
Iron-on bonded
parchment
Clear all-purpose, or
fabric, adhesive
A suitable lamp adapter

Method

Measure the lampshade frame and then cut a piece of parchment the same depth, but 1 in. longer than the measurement round the outside.

Iron the linen on to the bonded side of the parchment, trimming it level with the edge along one short side, but leaving 1 in. overlapping on the other three edges. Mitre the corners, then turn this surplus over and stick to reverse side of parchment.

Oversew the linen-covered parchment round the top and bottom of the frame and stick join (cut edge of linen underneath).

Fit lamp adapter as instructions.

The lampshades

Woven striped shade

I chose woven braids which picked up the colours and texture of the base. Yours will probably be different widths, and your shade possibly a different size, but I give my quantities and measurements as an indication—as I have done for all the shades. This should help you calculate your own materials, and also act as a guide in planning the proportions of your shade in relation to the size of the base.

Materials

2 8-in.-diameter
lampshade rings, one
with lamp fitting
White lampshade
parchment (7 ins. by
28 ins.)
1½ yds. 1½-in-wide woven
braid
3 yds. ½-in.-wide braid to
tone
Clear all-purpose, or
fabric, adhesive

Method

Cut the parchment carefully to the precise size you require (mine is 7 ins. deep)—the width should be the measurement round the ring, plus 1 in. for overlap.

Using double thread (I run mine through beeswax to prevent it breaking and knotting), oversew one long edge of the parchment round one of the rings, ending at beginning of overlap. Stitch the other edge to the second ring in the same way. Stick join, then oversew top and bottom of overlap.

Stick stripes of wide braid round shade as illustrated, 2 ins. apart. Then stick stripes of narrow braid between, finishing with the same braid round the upper and lower edges, as shown.

Random green wool shade

Multi-shaded knitting wool decorates this shade—toning perfectly with the horizontally-bound raffia base.

Method

Cut the parchment (my shade is 6 ins. deep), and oversew round rings and stick join as described for previous shade.

Make a knot at the end of the wool and stitch it securely to one edge of the shade: then wind the wool round and round the shade, criss-crossing, as illustrated. When you are satisfied with the effect, secure cut end at the edge of the shade as before.

To make the trimming, wind the wool evenly round and round $\frac{3}{8}$-in.-deep strips of parchment, so that it is completely covered. Stick round upper and lower edges of shade, as illustrated.

Lace striped shade

Bands of open-work lace are in perfect harmony with the delicate grass-heads of the lamp below. A narrower lace could trim the edges too, if preferred. The brown poplin ground is bonded to parchment as for the linen base.

Method

Cut the parchment to size (my shade is 6 ins. deep), and carefully iron the poplin on to the bonded side as described for the green linen lamp base, but trim edges level. Then oversew round rings and stick join as for first shade.

Stick ten vertical strips of lace at equal intervals round the shade, then stick braid or other trimming round the upper and lower edges.

Daisy-chain golden straw shade

An inexpensive woven straw table mat made this shade—bamboo would be just as good. And of course the trimming is a matter of choice: all sorts of alternatives suggest themselves (plain woven braid, plaited raffia, etc.), according to your choice of covering, and the lamp base.

Materials

2 6-in.-diameter
lampshade rings, one
with lamp fitting
White lampshade
parchment (5 ins. by
21 ins.)
Woven straw or bamboo
table mat to cover
1¼ yds. lace daisies (or
alternative trimming)
Clear all-purpose
adhesive

Method

Cut the parchment (my shade is 5 ins. deep), oversew round rings and stick join as described for the first shade. Then cut a strip of table mat the same depth as your shade and stick the top and bottom edges round the shade, on top of the parchment. If necessary, cut another piece to complete, over-lapping the edges of the straw at each side. Then catch neatly round top and bottom with tiny stitches.

Finally, stick trimming round upper and lower edges as illustrated.

Shiny green raffia shade

The slightly uneven covering of shiny green raffia creates a rather translucent, underwater appearance. Attractive at all times, like all these shades, it is at its most effective when the lamp is lit.

Materials

2 6-in.-diameter
lampshade rings, one
with lamp fitting
White lampshade
parchment (7 ins. by
21 ins., plus 2 strips
⅜ in. by 21 ins.)
Shiny green raffia
Clear all-purpose, or
fabric, adhesive

Method

Cut the parchment (my shade is 7 ins. deep), oversew round rings and stick join as described for the first shade.

Make a knot at the end of the raffia and stitch it securely to one edge of the shade: then wind the raffia evenly round and round the shade as illus-trated, until you reach the other edge. Secure cut end at the edge of the shade as before.

To make the trimming, wind the raffia evenly round and round ⅜-in.-deep strips of parchment, so that it is completely covered. Stick round upper and lower edges of shade, as illustrated.

The candles

All the candles pictured on page 57 are either the cheap white household kind, or else the most inexpensive plain coloured candles I could find. The secret of the "stained glass" and gold or silver "filigree" effects is simply children's inexpensive wax crayons!

The method is very easy and very quick. Just two brief warnings. *Do* buy good-quality crayons—it makes all the difference to your candles, though there is little difference in price: and *do* buy plenty of candles—once you start, you won't want to stop!

Materials

Candles (as above)
Children's wax crayons (in as wide a colour range as possible, as well as gold and silver)
A lighted candle to work with
A spare candle to experiment with
A gas match, battery lighter or similar flame (see below)

Method

First, spreading newspaper over your table-top, stand your working candle in a holder or mound of Plasticine, and light it.

Decide on your proposed colour scheme (study my examples as an indication). Then remove some of the paper covering the crayon and, with the candle you want to decorate in one hand, hold the end of the crayon briefly in the flame to melt it, and then quickly dab it against the side of the candle in your hand, so that it leaves a spot. Continue back and forth between candle and flame, just as you would apply sealing wax, until your candle is covered in dots of colour: it doesn't matter how untidy or uneven the spots are.

Now repeat the process with your second colour, dabbing it between the first spots, and finally add the third colour, so that the candle is fairly well covered with crayon. At this stage, it looks an irretrievable disaster!

It is wise to practise the next operation before beginning on your candle. I use the automatic match on my gas cooker, which I find ideal, but any similar jet of flame, or a cigarette lighter, would do—or you could even rotate the candle in front of an electric or gas fire (using tongs). Alternatively, you can continue with the candle you have been using—which will give a rather pleasing, slightly sooty effect, over the merged colours.

Holding the candle horizontally at one end, run the flame over the surface (or hold the candle near the heat), moving and rotating it gently all the time, until the colours begin to melt and run into each other: when this happens, move quickly to another area. You can always return to melt the spots a little more if necessary, but never stay too long in one place. Continue until the colours have merged satisfactorily over the entire surface of the candle. When cold, polish with a soft cloth.

This is the basic method for achieving the most

complex colour effects: the others are merely variations on the same theme. Here are the details.

A   The only three-colour "merged" combination: violet-blue, red-violet and carnation pink on a white candle.

B   Blue-violet and red-violet on a white candle.

C   Violet-red and carnation pink on a white candle.

D   Bands of colour on a white candle, beginning at the top with yellow, then yellow-orange, red-orange, red and finally violet-red.

E   Brown on a white candle.

F   Orange-red on a yellow candle.

G   Blue-violet on a pale blue candle: very thick near the base, gradually disappearing towards the top.

H   Violet-red on a pale pink candle: in this case I have made short abstract strokes and dabs of colour, and left them as they are.

J   Silver crayon on a purple candle—only lightly melted, so that it fuses to the surface.

K   A thick encrustation of gold on a household candle: only melt the surface sufficiently to prevent the gold falling away.

L   Tiny stones on a night-light.

The candleholders

If you want to make your own candle-stands to match your candles, here's a quick way. Simply fix the candle firmly and steadily in a lump of Plasticine, then press tiny coloured stones or chippings closely all over the surface (mine were originally intended for the aquarium!).

The honeycomb candle

This sweetly scented candle is the most nostalgic reminder I know of summer days in the country, and such a lovely thing to have and to burn that I couldn't resist the temptation to include it. Candle-making suppliers sell sheets of beeswax in natural and various colours. Simply lay a length of wick along one short edge of the sheet, then gently roll the beeswax up Swiss-roll fashion, round the wick (slightly warm the wax if necessary). Seal the join by slightly warming, trim the wick and coat with wax so that it will light.

56

6

Bear in mind

I had so many ideas for this chapter that I didn't know where to begin—or end! So the few designs I have shown are really only intended to inspire you with dozens more of your own.

Hessian webbing is a lovely basic belting material—and *so* cheap! It cries out to be decorated with brightly coloured embroidered ribbon, braid, lace or embroidered flowers, buttons, beads, sequins . . . anything which makes a striking contrast.

Fancy buttons make fabulous jewellery — they're often quite gem-like before you begin, and fixed to an unusual mount, make exciting pendants, brooches and ear-rings. Incidentally, I always prevent pendants twisting in wear by fixing a tiny safety pin at the back.

Wear it country style

Seven casual belts with jewellery to match

Big, bold belts to sling low round your hips—and country-bred jewellery with a slightly Pagan feeling. . . . Gay belts and fun jewellery are everyone's fashion favourites, so I've prettied a variety of rough, tough, homespun materials to make some stylish accessories which will add a distinctive touch to tweeds, sweaters and pants.

I have concentrated on the low-slung, hip-hugging style of casual belt—but it's only a matter of shortening if you want to wear any of these designs neatly at waist height. You'll want to decide your own length, anyway, so that the belts fit your hips comfortably. I have based mine on a standard 36 inches: try this with a tape measure and decide whether you want to alter the length—and if so, by how much. Then simply adjust my measurements accordingly.

The belts

Use real suede or leather—or cheat with an imitation: there are some excellent suede fabrics and shiny pvc materials available to make different versions of this striking belt.

Method

Cut the suede to size and the webbing to the correct length. Stick the webbing to the wrong side of the suede, so that it overlaps equally at each side. Turn over the surplus suede and stick to the webbing.

Cut three or four diamond shapes in a 2-in.-wide strip of ½-in.-squared, or graph, paper, following diagram overleaf carefully, so that they are 1 in. wide and 2 ins. apart.

Cowboy studded suede

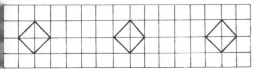

EACH SQUARE = ½"

Materials

A piece of suede, leather or fabric, 36 ins. by 4 ins.
1 yd. 2-in.-wide webbing
44 9-mm. gilt prong studs
A 3½-in.-diameter cork table mat
2 hooks and eyes
Fabric adhesive

Beginning 4 ins. from one end, place the paper on the right side of the belt, level with the edges, and mark the four corners of each diamond with a dot on the suede. Move the paper along, always aligning the first hole in the paper over the last marked diamond to ensure correct spacing. Continue along remainder of belt.

Now fix the studs in position. Begin with a small diamond, by placing each stud centrally over a dot. Then make a larger diamond by placing the inner prong of each stud over a dot, so that the studs are more widely spaced. Press the prongs firmly down inside the belt.

Stick the cork mat securely to one end of the belt. Trim the other end to meet underneath so that the diamonds are an equal distance away at each side (as illustrated), and stitch two hooks and eyes underneath to fasten.

Candy store

Materials

1 yd. 2-in.-wide webbing
1 yd. 2-in.-wide self-adhesive tape
Large coloured wooden beads (about 15)
Small coloured wooden beads (about 250)
A 3½-in.-diameter cork table mat
Linen carpet thread
2 hooks and eyes
Clear all-purpose, or fabric, adhesive

Brightly coloured wooden beads remind me of an old-fashioned sweet shop—and in this gay, amusing belt they are just as tempting!

Method

Beginning 1½ ins. from the end, mark the right side of the webbing every 3 ins., ½ in. below the edge. Leave 3–4 ins. free at the other end.

Stitch a large bead at each marked point, so that the hole in the bead runs along the belt (see diagram below.

Thread a needle with a piece of carpet thread about 60 ins. long, and stitch securely at one side of the first bead. Pass the thread through the bead, then thread on about twenty small beads before passing it through the next large fixed bead. Check that the loop is the required length (see picture) and add more beads if necessary. Then continue along length of belt, using the same number of small beads for each loop. Finish off securely.

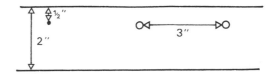

Thread four strings of small beads, each ending with a large one, so that they hang from the centre of the cork mat (take the thread from the back to the front of the mat, pass through the small beads, loop through the large one, then take the thread up the small ones again and through to the back of the mat). Stick the mat to one end of the belt, level with the last large bead. Adjust the other end of the belt so that the ends meet underneath, with the last large bead level with the mat, matching the other side. Stitch two hooks and eyes underneath to fasten.

Stick adhesive tape to inside of belt to stiffen the webbing.

Pretty patches

Patchwork is such a well-loved tradition that I felt it was a "must" for this collection of belts. I chose a selection of the famous Liberty printed lawns—these are all taken from the original old blocks which were used at the beginning of this century, and have only just been re-discovered.

Materials

1 yd. 2½-in.-wide hessian webbing
Scraps of fine printed cotton
Thin paper
24 ins. lacing cord in each of four colours.

Method

First make your patches. Trace the hexagon shape below) and cut it absolutely accurately in thin card to use as a template. Draw round this to cut about twelve hexagons in thin paper.

Pin these to the wrong side of your fabric, positioning carefully so that the design will fall attractively on your patch, then cut the fabric about ¼ in. larger all round. Turn the surplus fabric neatly over the edge of the paper, one side at a time, and tack to hold in place.

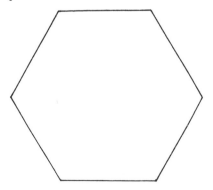

Beginning about 2 ins. from one end, pin the patches into position on the hessian, about $\frac{1}{8}$ in. from the edge, and $\frac{1}{2}$ in. apart. Adjust if necessary, then oversew neatly into place with tiny stitches. Remove tacking threads.

Turn under the raw edge of the hessian at each end and stitch. Cut cord into 12-in. lengths: knot one end and sew the other securely inside the end of the belt, so that the four pairs of cords are joined to the belt as illustrated. Catch them together at each side to make the fastening neater when knotted.

Rondo

Rosy raffia rings decorate a rough hessian belt: what could be simpler!

Method

Buttonhole neatly all round each curtain ring with raffia: finish off, but *do not cut remaining raffia.*

Beginning about 4 ins. from one end, mark the hessian with a pin every 2½ ins. Stitch the required number of rings into position centrally over each of these points, using the surplus raffia still joined to the ring.

Buttonhole closely round the buckle in the same way, then stitch to one end of the belt and stick the corners of the other end back to form a point, as illustrated.

Materials

1 yd. 2-in.-wide hessian webbing
12 ¾-in.-diameter plastic curtain rings
1 2-in.-diameter round belt buckle
shiny raffia
Fabric adhesive

Coffee and cream lace

Heavy, unbleached Cluny lace makes this feminine belt with its pretty front fastening. The clotted cream colour of the lace is beautifully contrasted by the coffee tone underneath.

Materials

1 yd. 2-in.-wide webbing
1 yd. 2-in.-wide heavy lace
1 yd. 2-in.-wide self-adhesive tape
24 ins. 1-in.-wide braid
2 hooks and eyes

Method

Place the lace over the webbing, so that it is absolutely flat, and pin. Then stitch neatly along the upper and lower edges. Turn under and stitch the raw edge at each end, so that the pattern of the lace corresponds. Stitch two hooks and eyes to fasten. Stick tape to inside of belt to stiffen the webbing.

Cut off a 2-in. length of braid, then fold the remainder as diagram left, and gather tightly as indicated by broken line, to form a bow. Fold the 2-in. strip lengthways into three, then bind tightly round gathered centre of bow and join ends neatly at the back. Stitch bow securely to one end of belt, as illustrated.

67

Plaited girdle

Choose three toning, but well-defined, shades of heavy cord for this quickie girdle that might have been worn by Queen Guinevere or some equally aristocratic medieval lady!

Materials

1½ yds. in each of three shades of silk dressing-gown cord
Hook and eye

Method

Bind one end of each length of cord tightly with matching cotton about ½ in. from the cut end, to prevent fraying.

Place these three ends together and knot tightly 6 ins. from the cut ends.

Plait neatly and evenly to within 6 ins. of the other end, then knot tightly again.

Trim ends to length, then bind tightly with cotton as before.

Stitch hook and eye to knots to fasten.

Tapestry money minder

Canvas-work is a most absorbing and relaxing pastime—but it's wise not to take on anything too ambitious to begin with, or it may prove too much. There's just the right amount of work here to give you a taste for tapestry—and produce a belt in subtle shades, that incorporates a novel (and useful) purse. I have used cross-stitch, to give a close, hard-wearing finish.

Materials

Double-thread canvas—
10 stitches to the inch
(see below for sizes of pieces)
Tapestry wool in four muted shades (I chose wine, deep rose, pink and beige)
A piece of stiff buckram
A 4-inch zip
2 hooks and eyes
Fabric adhesive

Method

On a piece of canvas about 3½ ins. square, work the buckle, following diagram a, in cross-stitch (make sure all your stitches cross in the same direction).

On another piece of canvas, 5 ins. wide by 6 ins. deep, work the design following diagram b—positioning it ½ in. from the top, with an equal amount of free canvas at each side. When this is complete, work an equal area, plus ½ in. in depth, directly below the patterned piece—in plain wine (or your darkest colour): this forms the back of the purse.

Following diagram c, work a strip of about 30 ins. long for the belt, allowing about ¾ in. of free canvas along each side (this can be worked in two pieces and joined).

BUCKLE

+ Wine
O Deep Rose
X Pink
• Beige

BELT

c

b

PURSE

To make up, back the buckle with buckram, then mitre the corners of the surplus canvas and stick to the back of the buckram.

Right side inside, fold the purse between the bottom row of the pattern and the first row of plain back. Join each side neatly, close to the embroidery, matching the squares in the canvas. Trim seams and turn to right side. Stitch one side of the zip along the top front edge of the purse, then stitch the other side to the lower edge of the belt, 2 ins. from the end.

Turn back and stitch the excess canvas along the lower edge of the belt (including the top of the purse). Then turn the excess along the top edge over, stitch and stick the edge.

Join one end of the belt to the side of the buckle, finish the other end neatly and fasten with hooks and eyes.

The jewellery

Chamois and wood choker

An ordinary chamois wash leather, studded with dark, polished wooden beads, makes a most alluring "dog collar" to wear with plain sweaters.

Method

Cut the petersham a little shorter than the measurement round your neck. Cut a strip of chamois the same length, but overlapping $\frac{3}{8}$ in. along each side (making it about $1\frac{3}{8}$ ins. wide).

Stick the petersham down the centre of the wrong side of the chamois, then turn the surplus over each edge and stick to the back of the petersham.

Beginning about $1\frac{1}{2}$ ins. from the end, mark the chamois at $\frac{1}{2}$-in. intervals, then stitch a bead at each of these points.

Finally, cut two 4-in.-long "strings" of chamois, first folding it over and sticking to make it double, then cutting quite close to the fold. Knot one end of each string and stitch the other inside the end of the choker, with a bead on top.

Materials

Chamois leather (as above) or suede
12 ins. $\frac{5}{8}$-in.-wide petersham ribbon
20 small wooden beads
Fabric adhesive

Stringalong

An abstract design worked in fine cord on dark brown petersham: you let the string form its own pattern as you sew, for this unusual "slave" band.

Method

Cut the petersham the same length as your neck measurement, then turn under $\frac{1}{2}$ in. at each end.

Beginning 6 ins. from the end of the piping cord, stitch it, using matching cotton, to the end of the

70

petersham—so that the free 6 ins. of cord overlaps the end of the ribbon to form a tie. Now, continue to stitch the cord to the ribbon, allowing it to twist and turn and curl round to form an abstract design as you sew, "couching" the cord neatly into position along its length. To couch, bring the needle up underneath the cord, take the matching cotton round it and then take the needle back through the petersham underneath, so that the cord is held by the loop of thread.

Continue in this way until you reach the other end of the ribbon, then finish with a 6-in. tie as at the beginning.

This method is equally suitable for a more formal design, of course: a lattice of zig-zag pattern could be worked in contrasting colours or weights of cord.

Materials

12 ins. 1-in.-wide petersham ribbon
1½ yds. narrow piping cord

Daisy band

Just a chain of guipure lace daisies on a contrasting band of petersham. But the decoration could be any pretty lace or braid—and the colours teamed to partner a favourite dress.

Materials

12 ins. ⅝-in.-wide petersham ribbon
12 ins. lace daisies or similar trimming
12 ins. Russian braid

Method

Cut the petersham the same length as your neck measurement, then turn under ½ in. at each end.

Cut the Russian braid into two 6-in. lengths and stitch one inside each end of the ribbon to form ties.

Stitch the lace daisies or alternative decoration neatly along the length of the ribbon, using matching cotton.

Pagan pendants

Plain sweaters cry out for an eye-catching pendant— and it's fun to ring the changes with an intriguing collection. Here are three examples—all made in exactly the same way—to show different interpretations of the same design. I used chamois and suede to make the mounts for my versions, but leather, hessian, velvet, fine corduroy—the possibilities for interesting covering materials are endless. And you only need visit your nearest button counter for your central inspiration!

Method

Cut a circle of card the size required (mine are 2½ ins. and 2 ins. in diameter). Make a hole in the centre.

Stick wadding to one side of card. Trim so that it just fractionally overlaps the edge of the card. Cut away a hole in the centre (about ½-in. diameter).

Stick the card circle, wadding side down, lightly to the wrong side of the chamois or alternative material for the mount. Cut the chamois so that it overlaps the card ½ in. all round. Snip this surplus all the way round so that it forms tiny tabs (stop slightly short of the edge of the card). Turn these tabs neatly over and stick to the back of the card.

Make sure that the shank of your button fits snugly into the centre of the mount, then stick into position with all-purpose adhesive.

Cut a circle of chamois or alternative, slightly smaller than the mount, and stick neatly over the back.

Stitch thong, cord, etc., to back, to hang.

Materials

Chamois, suede, leather, etc., for mount
A decorative button
Wadding
Stiff card
A leather thong, lacing cord, Russian braid, etc., to hang (about 1 yd. long)
Fabric adhesive
Clear all-purpose adhesive

Raffia and bead pendant

Materials

Shiny raffia
A string of wooden beads (about 24 ins. long)
5 coloured wooden beads
Stiff card

Shiny, straw-coloured raffia is matched by natural wooden beads—and contrasted by a few vibrant ones: just like poppies in a cornfield!

Method

Cut a 2½-in.-diameter circle of stiff card, with a ¾-in.-diameter hole in the centre.

Buttonhole closely all round the circle, so that the card is completely covered.

Make a knot at the end of a piece of raffia. Thread on a coloured bead, then attach to the bottonholed edge of the circle by passing the needle through from the back to the front—and back again through the next hole: thread on another bead, knot the raffia and cut—making sure there is just enough "play" to allow the beads to hang freely. Attach two more beads in the same way, and a final single one.

Join a long piece of raffia to the edge opposite the beads in the same way (from back to front and back again): then thread both ends through a single bead before dividing and threading an equal number of beads on each half. Knot raffia close to last bead to prevent slipping.

Victorian echoes

I am a compulsive rummager amongst Victorian bric-à-brac. And since it is obvious that many people share my delight in what has become known as "Victoriana", I make no apology for this miscellany of things which might have charmed great-grandmama.

Though I must hasten to add that it would quickly shatter all her illusions to discover what wicked fakes they are (which means that anyone can make them at little expense!). The "antique silver" cross and "beaten pewter" frame are kitchen foil, the bell jars are cheap drinking glasses, the delicate filigree design on the pottery is the work of a moment with a modern plastic cake doily—even home-made pot-pourri can be assured of success with the addition of a modern biological product.

Miniature bell jars

A delicate dried flower arrangement protected in clear glass—evocative of the large bell jars so beloved by the Victorians. These are less cumbersome—just the right size for a coffee table or bookshelf decoration. And they make an exquisite gift.

Method

Turn the glass upside-down on a piece of stiff card: draw round the rim and cut out.

Roll a ball of plasticine the size of a walnut. Squeeze a little adhesive in the centre of the card, then press the plasticine down on to it so that it forms a mound with a flat base. Leave to dry.

Decide the colour scheme you plan to follow (don't mix too many colours—concentrate on two or three for an artistic effect): then push the tallest,

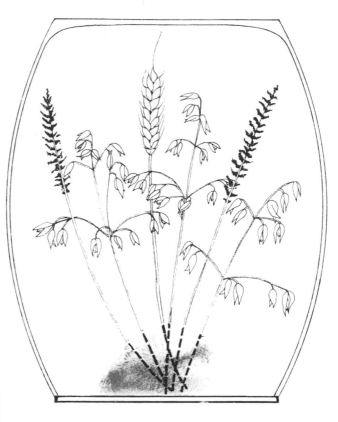

Materials

Dried flowers, grasses,
oats, statice, etc., as
available
A clear drinking glass
(about 4 or 5 ins.
high)
Plasticine (white or
stone)
Stiff card
Narrow braid or velvet
ribbon to trim
(optional)
Felt for base
Silica gel crystals
(available from
chemists)
Clear adhesive tape
Clear all-purpose
adhesive

central piece of your arrangement (I usually make this a grass-head or ear of barley) down into the top of the plasticine. Place the glass over it to check for height and position.

Then, constantly checking the effect inside the glass, continue to add pieces of grass, oats, etc., and flowers (I used glixia), working downwards and outwards as illustrated. Finish with more flower-heads pushed into the base of the plasticine, so that it is completely hidden (I used statice for this).

When you are satisfied with the arrangement, spread a little adhesive on the card base and sprinkle some silica gel crystals over it: this prevents moisture forming inside the sealed glass.

Polish the glass well inside and out, then pick up and gently lower the upturned arrangement into the glass. Check the position, then stick the base into position with clear tape, half ot it covering the rim of the glass, the remainder overlapping: snip this into tabs and stick neatly to the underside of the card.

Stick trimming round rim of glass if required.

Cut a piece of felt the same size as the base, and stick underneath to neaten.

Antique silver cross

Make this, or a circular or abstract-shaped design, as a brooch, ear-rings or pendant. The beaten silver or pewter appearance is most deceptive—it's achieved with string and cooking foil—and a touch of black ink!

Method

Trace the outline from the diagram below and cut in stiff card.

Stick cord or string to the surface of the card, all round, level with the edge. Then cut four 1-in. lengths, form into tear-drop shapes and stick to each

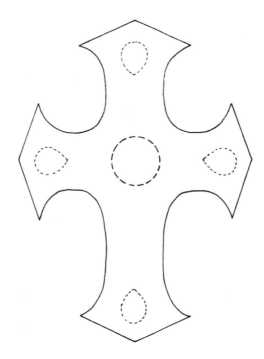

Materials

Stiff card
Narrow piping cord or heavy string
Silver cooking foil
Black ink (or enamel paint)
Fine chain to hang (or brooch back, etc.)
Clear all-purpose, or fabric, adhesive

arm of the cross as indicated. Finally, cut a $1\frac{1}{2}$-in. length and stick in a circle in the centre.

With the dull side uppermost, press a piece of foil gently down over the card, allowing it to crease into and around the raised design. Lift off carefully, spread some adhesive over the surface of the card and then replace foil. Cut away foil, leaving $\frac{1}{2}$ in. all round. Snip this surplus and stick the resulting tabs to the back of the cross. Then stick another piece of foil over the back of the cross and trim edge level all round.

Finally, soak a small piece of cotton wool in black ink or paint and dab over the surface of the foil, picking out the design by allowing it to collect in the crevices, but smearing it elsewhere. Leave to dry.

Fix chain to hang (fix a tiny safety pin at the back to prevent it twisting)—or stick brooch back, etc., at back if making alternative version.

Pewter horseshoe flower frame

The "antique" frame which prettily displays a tiny arrangement of fresh or dried flowers is made in just the same way. If using fresh flowers, fix a small foil container behind filled with damp florists' material —or water: lily-of-the-valley, violets and a single pink rosebud with a few fern fronds make a lovely picture. Dried flowers can be tied in a bunch and fixed at the back with tape.

Materials

Stiff card
Various thicknesses of piping cord or string
Silver cooking foil
Black ink (or enamel paint)
Clear all-purpose, or fabric, adhesive

Method

Following the directions on page 48 for drawing an oval, but substituting the following measurements, draw out the shape on your card:

A–B = 8 ins. (A–D, D–C, etc., each measure 2 ins.)
E–F = 3 ins.

Now, following diagram 48, rule the 4-in. horizontal line J–K. And with centre C, draw a 2-in.-diameter circle.

Cut round the edge of the oval, ending with the straight lower edge J–K. Cut out the centre circle.

Stick different thicknesses of cord or string to form a raised pattern on the surface of the card, as for the cross. I used thick piping cord level with the edge, followed by three more graduating thicknesses inside, each touching the last: then a wavy line of medium-thickness cord all round the curved part of the frame.

Smooth a piece of foil over (shiny side down), stick, finish round the inner and outer edges, and "antique" with black ink or paint, exactly as described for the cross.

Fix a strut at the back to stand.

Bell book and candle

"Pottery" is an easy matter if you use a self-hardening modelling material—and very satisfying. The old-fashioned-looking bells and candlestick are simply thin sheets of the material rolled out like pastry and cut to shape. Dampen the clay slightly if it becomes too dry while you are working—and I use talcum powder to "flour" the board and prevent the rolling pin (which can be a smooth-sided bottle) from sticking.

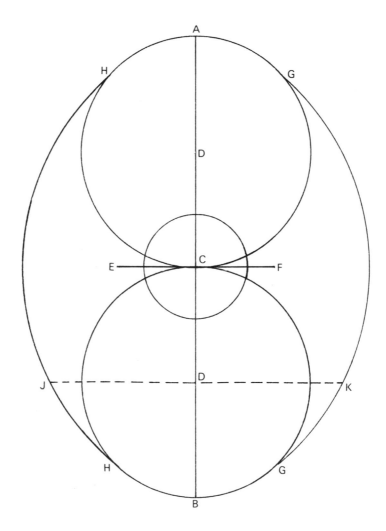

The candlestick

Method

Roll out a piece of clay to form a circle about $4\frac{1}{2}$ ins. in diameter and $\frac{3}{8}$ in. thick.

Sprinkle the surface liberally with talcum powder, then lay the lace doily right side down on top. Roll across the back of the doily until it is evenly pressed right in, making sure it does not shift as you roll. Carefully lift and remove the doily. Then, following the pattern, cut out a circle, about 4 ins. in diameter, using a sharp knife. Neaten the cut edge all the way round.

Roll out and decorate another piece of clay and cut a strip about 5 ins. long and $1\frac{1}{4}$ ins. wide (a fraction longer than is necessary to go round your candle). Form into a circle, join the sides with water, reinforcing with a narrow strip inside. Then dampen the lower edge and press firmly on to the base, pushing a narrow strip of wet clay well into the angle of the join all round the inside.

When quite dry and hard, paint and varnish as required.

Materials

Self-hardening modelling material
A small plastic cake doily (choose a fairly thick one, with a clearly defined cut-out lace pattern)
Talcum powder
Poster paint and clear varnish (or enamel paint)

The bells

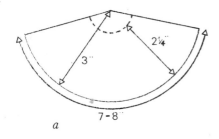

a

b

These are made on exactly the same principle as the candlestick, but the clay is rolled rather thinner, and only half the doily (mine was 6 ins. in diameter) is needed to make the pattern.

Having rolled out and decorated the clay as previously described, cut a "fan" shape to the measurements in diagram *a*, and remove the centre as indicated by the broken line.

Bend round into a cone, dampen and join the edges and reinforce with a strip of wet clay inside, as before. Then gently press into a bell shape as illustrated—spreading out the lower edge or not, as desired.

Make a small handle, as shown in diagram *b*, and thread a short piece of wire through it, as indicated.

Lower through the hole at the top of the bell, dampen the edge, then press in and join to the handle. Make a simple design on the handle with the point of a knitting needle or similar object.

When quite dry and hard, paint and varnish as required—and fix a tiny bell to the wire inside.

The Victorian book-mark

The Victorians loved books, so they needed book-marks—and these, of course, were another excuse for lavish decoration. I have used velvet ribbon with a pattern of seed pearls based on guipure lace daisies. But my design should serve only as an example: moiré or satin ribbon would be equally suitable, and any pretty lace could form the basis for a pattern of tiny coloured beads, sequins, etc.—or you could use a fine braid. The arrangement you will find dictated by your own choice of materials—and your imagination.

Materials

12 ins. 1¼–1½-in.-wide ribbon
12 ins. toning (double-edge) lace or braid
24 ins. narrow lace to edge (optional)
Pearls, beads, sequins, etc.
Fabric adhesive

Method

Turn under and stick the raw edge at each end of the ribbon. Then stick or stitch the toning lace down the centre.

Using the lace as a basis for your design, stitch pearls, beads, sequins, etc., over and beside it as illustrated, decorating the bottom attractively with a fringe, tassel or as shown.

Stick narrow lace to the back of the ribbon so that it overlaps the side edges as illustrated.

Roses and forget-me-not paperweights

The typically Victorian "china" paperweight is made with the same modelling material as the bells and candlestick. Although it looks much more complicated, the flowers are, in fact, very simple to make—requiring care and patience rather than great skill. Follow the diagrams, working with fairly dry clay, but keeping the separate petals under a damp cloth as you prepare them before assembling each rose.

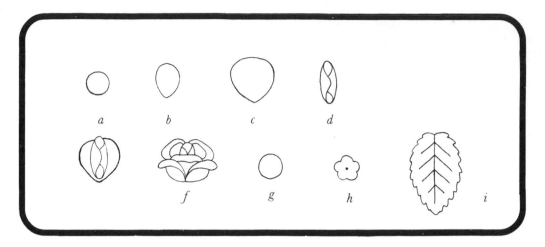

I use water colours in a white poster colour or gouache base to paint the flowers. Paint each flower and leaf separately before mounting together on the base. Then coat with clear varnish.

Method

Roll some modelling clay into a tiny ball, then flatten it and gently shape into a petal—following diagrams *a*, *b* and *c* (these are roughly actual size—though you can adapt the method to any size you wish, remembering that larger flowers will need more petals). Make four petals in this way: then roll one petal round as diagram *d* for the centre. Join another petal at the base, as diagram *e*, followed by the other two, so that the centre is surrounded. Curl the top of each petal back slightly, as illustrated.

Now make four more petals, slightly larger than the first. Join these evenly round the base of the rose, and curl the petals back as before, emphasising the curl of the previous petals at the same time. Slice away part of the back of the rose to form a flat base (diagram *f*). Leave to dry and harden.

To make the forget-me-nots, flatten an even tinier ball of clay, and then make five indentations round the edge (I used a pin), to form petals. Make a small indentation at the centre (I used the head of the pin for this)—see diagrams *g* and *h*.

Make the leaves in the same way, making a serrated edge (I did this with my thumb-nail), and marking the veins with a knife (diagram *i*). Curl over before leaving to dry.

Roll a ball of clay for the base, then flatten to form

required shape (the one in the illustration is just over 1½ ins. in diameter). Leave to harden and thoroughly dry out.

Paint the flowers, leaves and base as described at the beginning and, when dry, stick into position with clear all-purpose adhesive. I painted my three roses deep crimson, dusky pink and cream, set a yellow-green leaf (the edges slightly tinged with crimson) between, and then flanked each rose with three blue forget-me-not heads.

Finish with a coat of clear gloss varnish.

The scents of summer

As I mentioned earlier, down the centuries it has been found—at first necessary, then desirable and later pleasantly nostalgic, to dry flower petals in order to preserve their perfume. Pot-pourri—as this mixture which brings the garden indoors is called—filled pomander balls, china jars and open bowls: originally to combat unpleasant odours and later just to perfume the home, keep moths away, and scent fresh linen sweetly.

Pot-pourri was known to the Romans. But by Elizabethan times its making was an important part in the craft of housewifery. Most recipes were based on rose petals, mixed with a host of other ingredients, including sweet-smelling oils and spices, and allowed to ferment. The Victorians and Edwardians considered pot-pourri making an art too, and treasured their closely guarded favourite recipes. These were just as complicated and tricky as the earlier ones, needing a variety of expensive ingredients.

An old recipe for "Pot-pourri for a Parlour" (you used different ones for different rooms) called for damask roses, Province or House roses, syringa, clove pinks, rosemary leaves, myrtle, jessamine, lemon thyme, lavender, phlox, marigold, mint, bay leaves, lemon rind, nutmeg and cloves, orris root and bay-salt . . . in carefully proportioned quantities. The flowers had to be dried and then everything mixed together in the autumn, grating the nutmeg and crunching in the salt as one worked.

Not many people would want to go to so much trouble nowadays—especially when one can buy the most delightful genuine pot-pourri ready-made. I prefer to do this, then put in into jars and sachets to use in the old-fashioned way.

Pot-pourri perfume jar

Alternatively, there is a "pot-pourri maker" additive on the market now, which provides all the necessary flower oils, spices and fixatives in a tube. By adding this mixture to your own blend of rose, pansy, marigold, delphinium, nasturtium or other petals, you are assured of success.

Lavender, on the other hand, is an easy matter. Just gather the spikes as they ripen and allow to dry in the usual way. The flower-heads will readily fall away when thoroughly dried, and are then ready for use.

I fill old-fashioned "apothecary" glass storage jars with ready-made pot-pourri—then fancy them up with ribbons and artificial or dried flowers (the rose-buds in the picture are part of the pot-pourri).

A lidded china jar—or sometimes a box—was the customary method of using pot-pourri in the home in the eighteenth century. It would be placed near the fire in the evening until it was warm—when the lid would be taken off so that the delicate fragrance escaped to scent the whole room.

Lavender sachets

They used to be made of fine muslin trimmed with hand-made lace. But my lavender and pot-pourri sachets are in more practical nylon organdie, with machine-made nylon lace. Nevertheless, they still smell just as sweet!

Materials

(for each sachet)
Two 2½-in. squares of nylon organdie
¼ yd. ½-in.-wide gathered lace
3½ ins. narrow velvet or satin ribbon, lace motif or artificial flower spray to trim
Dried lavender or pot-pourri

Method

Stitch the gathered lace all round one piece of fabric, *on the right side*, ¼ in. from the edge, with the decorative edge towards the centre of the square. Tack the two pieces of fabric together, right sides inside, then join along three sides, following the previous stitching line. Trim seams, clip corners and turn to the right side.

Fill with lavender or pot-pourri, then turn in the remaining raw edges and slip-stitch together.

Make a tiny ribbon bow and stitch this or alternative trimming at one corner of the sachet.

The days are dull and misty, the ground is damp, and the chill air sends one scurrying indoors to curl up in front of the fire. As the year ends there is little to cheer the spirits—except the prospect of Christmas and the goodwill it inspires.

The shops are tinsel-draped and brightly lit, filled to bursting with irresistible goodies. Lists of presents are compiled and checked, Christmas shopping is a crazy, bustling rush, cards are written and received, and exciting smells escape from the kitchen. We look fondly at the red-breasted robin hopping cheerfully outside the window, and dream of deep white un-trodden snowdrifts . . . exclaiming in horrified surprise if it actually happens, and we find ourselves wading ankle-deep in dirty slush!

So we bring nature indoors—bunches of holly and mistletoe, trails of ivy, fir cones—and the Christmas tree itself, decorated with shiny coloured baubles and topped by a single silver star. A holly wreath welcomes friends at the front door . . . and in most churches and many homes, a traditional crib re-creates the Nativity scene. We have Saint Francis of Assisi to thank for this: he first encouraged villagers to re-enact the birth of Christ with live actors and animals. Then the custom developed of representing the characters with carved and painted wooden figures: a charming tradition which has survived the centuries to enjoy a popular revival today.

Here is my contribution to Christmas: very personal cards—and your own Nativity scene. May the beauty of Christmas inspire you throughout the coming year, as nature gradually re-awakens in the spring sunshine, and the cycle of life and growth begins all over again.

✂ Bear in mind

I have deliberately left all these greetings cards un-lettered, so that you can write your own message inside. But if you want to include a wish in the outer design—or give a really professional touch to the inside—it's easily added with rub-down lettering.

You can buy alphabet sheets in a wide variety of sizes and scripts from most stationers, and it's the easiest thing in the world to spell out your message. I always draw a very faint guide line to ensure my letters are absolutely level, and use the smooth point of a steel knitting needle for small print: you can use something bigger for larger letters, of course.

Remember to rub over the finished wording, covering it first with the special paper provided, to "set" your work—otherwise it may tend to peel off.

Greetings cards

for all occasions

It is always a pleasure to receive a card and know that somebody is thinking of one—whether it is celebrating a birthday or similar anniversary, or to wish one well or offer congratulations. So although I have designed some of the cards specifically for Christmas, others are equally suitable for any occasion throughout the year: these all use flowers, the universal language, arranged as miniature collages. Indeed, the recipient may well decide your card is something more—a gift, to be mounted and framed. . . . It's sure to be far too pretty to be hidden away unseen, or destroyed!

Hand-made cards are so personal—yet with clever use of colour and simple designs tastefully carried out, you can achieve the most professional results. I begin by using heavy paper in a strong colour—contrasted to those of my design. Then I work out the composition and arrangement before mounting anything down. This ensures a clean, neat result.

By the way, some of the more delicate flower cards should be packed in a shallow box, or well-protected, if they are to be sent through the post.

a

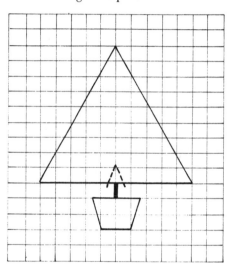

Be-ribbonned bouquet

A tall card (8 ins. by 4 ins.) with a side-fold, in pale lilac. Green dyed grass forms the background to the flowers—three or four separate sprays are stuck into position with all-purpose clear adhesive as for the collage pictures in Chapter 4. The flowers are glixia in three toning colours—deep blue, violet and pink—

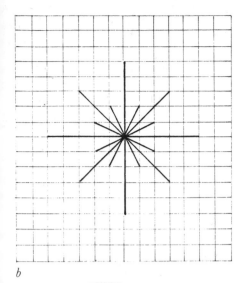

b

Raffia snowflake

about eight heads of each. The stems are tied together tightly with cotton, then the heads slipped up and down to form a satisfactory arrangement, as illustrated. This is laid flat on the grass and stitched to the card over the bound stems. The heads can be stuck with clear adhesive, to hold them in place. Trim the stems level, about an inch below the cotton.

Cut a small vertical slit in the paper at each side of the cotton: thread narrow satin ribbon through, tie in a bow over the stems, trim ends to length and catch down with adhesive as shown.

I used a shiny raffia in harvest gold—but natural would be equally effective. A dark background is essential: I chose olive green. The card is 4 ins. by $3\frac{1}{2}$ ins., with a side-fold.

Cut your paper to size, then take a piece of $\frac{1}{4}$-in.-squared paper the same size and rule out the star, following diagram *a*. Place this over your paper, edges level, and prick through it with a pin to mark the end of each line, and the centre.

Thread a tapestry needle with raffia, knot the end, and stitch the four longest lines between the outer end and the centre. Follow with the four shorter lines and then the eight very short ones: finally, stitch over the four longest lines again, finishing off securely at the back.

Stick a piece of thin paper over the back to neaten.

Christmas tree

Shiny green raffia makes a life-like tree on an orange ground 4 ins. by $3\frac{1}{2}$ ins., with a side-fold.

Rule out the design on a piece of $\frac{1}{4}$-in.-squared paper, following diagram *b* (ignore broken lines). Then trace the triangular tree shape and cut in thin paper.

Cut a short piece of raffia and bend into an upturned V-shape. Stick this at the centre of the base, overlapping the edge, as indicated by the broken line. Cut another piece of raffia, slightly longer, fold in half and stick round the outside of the first piece, so close that it covers the edge. Continue in this way, making each piece of raffia slightly longer than the last, until the ends begin to overlap the sides of the triangle: then cut them as illustrated, until the top is reached. Trim the lower edge neatly.

Place your squared pattern over your coloured paper, edges level, and prick the corners of the tree, the tub and position of the trunk.

Stick two or three short pieces of brown raffia together to form the trunk, then stick into position on the card, ends overlapping tree and tub. Stick the raffia-covered paper into place.

Cut the tub in red felt or paper, and stick into position.

Floral Noel

Emerald green makes a good background for the brightly-coloured glixia heads spelling out the message. The card measures 3 ins. by 8 ins., with a top-fold.

On a piece of $\frac{1}{4}$-in.-squared paper the same size as the card, mark the letters, following the diagram. Place this over your paper, edges level, and prick with a pin to mark the ends of each straight line and the curves of the O. Then rule in the lines on the paper for guidance.

Using clear all-purpose adhesive, stick the flower-heads close together to cover the lines. It is wise to experiment, arranging each line first, before laying a trail of adhesive over the pencil mark and pressing the flower-heads into it. Begin and end with a light colour.

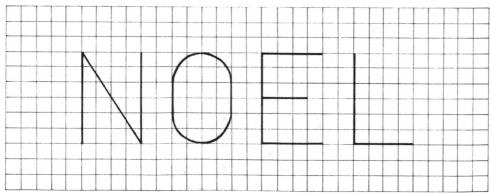

EACH SQUARE = ¼"

Informal flower arrangement

This simple, horizontal design (3½ ins. by 8 ins., with a top-fold) in pale blue, is made up just like the collages in Chapter 4.

Natural grass is stuck along the base and at one side. A few purple oats fall above some blue statice heads, with a bunch of pink glixia below. A straw-daisy covers the ends neatly in the corner.

90

Away in a manger

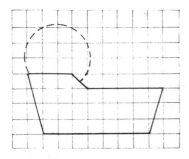

The simplicity of the crib is emphasised in a striking collage. Thin sheet balsa wood (available from model-makers' shops), grass-heads and sequins on a dark brown card $3\frac{1}{2}$ ins. by $4\frac{1}{2}$ ins., with a top-fold.

On a sheet of $\frac{1}{4}$-in.-squared paper, draw the crib, following the diagram. Cut out and use as a pattern to cut the shape in very thin balsa (1/32 in. or 1/16 in. thick), using a sharp craft knife.

Stick a tiny piece of grass seed-head to the back of the wood, so that the tip appears above the crib as illustrated. Then stick the balsa into position on the card, with tiny bits of heavier grass-head below.

91

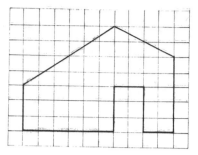

Mark a faint circle, about 1 in. in diameter, over the head of the crib, following the diagram. Then stick or stitch tiny gold sequins round the line (I stitched them, anchoring with a small gold bead at the centre).

Star of wonder, Star of light

A dramatic card in dark blue, 6 ins. by $3\frac{1}{2}$ ins., with a side-fold. I surrounded a diamanté centre with silver sequins in two sizes, and tiny glass beads. But this can be determined by what you have available: graduated seed pearls would make an ideal alternative.

Rule two faint pencil lines to form a cross, with the centre $1\frac{1}{2}$ ins. from the top and $1\frac{1}{4}$ ins. from the left-hand side edge. Stitch the largest bead or sequin at the centre, then stitch the remainder to form the horizontal and vertical lines of the cross (I stitched one large sequin above and at each side of the diamanté, and three below. Then two smaller sequins above and at each side, with four below, followed by a string of tiny glass beads—which I also used to anchor the sequins). Finish with another smaller bead or sequin in each angle at the centre. The completed cross should measure $1\frac{1}{2}$ ins. by $3\frac{1}{2}$ ins.

Stick a length of narrow lace behind the right-hand edge of the card.

Sweet and simple collage

A narrow, vertical card (6 ins. by 3 ins.) with a side-fold—but it would be equally effective as a horizontal design with a top-fold.

I have used feathery brown grass-heads on a gold ground, with a crimson straw-daisy at the centre, surrounded by bright green and yellow dyed flower-heads.

Use clear all-purpose adhesive, arranging and mounting in the usual way.

Silent Night

This simple, yet artistic, card (6 ins. by 5½ ins., with a side-fold), combines three previous methods on a deep violet ground.

Draw and cut the stable in thin balsa wood as for the crib, following the diagram. Stick a piece of black paper behind the cut-out doorway.

Stick into position on the card, then stick several lengths of natural raffia to form each side of the sloping roof (cut them 2½ ins. and 1¾ ins. long respectively). Stick a grass seed-head at one side to form a tree.

Make a simpler version of the star described previously, positioning the centre 1½ ins. from both top and side edges. Finished, it should measure 1¼ ins. by 1¾ ins.

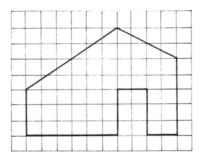

Once in royal David's city

Nothing is more traditional than a Nativity scene in the form of a Christmas crib. Children love to see the familiar story brought to life—the humble Holy Family, and the three Kings, resplendent in their royal robes. For grown-ups, it is an essential part of the festivities, reminding us of the true meaning of Christmas.

I have tried to design a crib which is striking in its simplicity. Only basic, easily obtained, materials are used—mainly paper and wood. The figures are as simple as possible in their construction, their effect relying solely on draped paper table napkins soaked in wallpaper paste. The stable is balsa wood (obtainable from model-makers' shops)—which is easily cut with a sharp knife and a metal-edged rule.

Method

To make the kings, draw an 8-in.-diameter circle on the buckram, with a ½-in.-diameter circle in the centre. Divide this circle into three equal sections,

Materials

5 1-in.-diameter
wooden balls
1 ¾-in.-diameter
wooden ball
Hat buckram
2- or 3-ply tissue soft
paper table napkins
in brown, blue, white
and assorted colours
for the kings
Foil or decorative
coloured paper in
three shades
Small piece of plain
brown paper
Knitting wool
Cotton wool
Scrap of gilt braid
(optional)
Diamanté or similar
jewels (optional)
Cocktail sticks or pipe
cleaners
Garden raffia
2 36-in.-long by 3-in.-
wide strips of balsa
wood, ⅛ in. thick
Tiny pins
Adhesive tape
Wallpaper paste
Fabric adhesive
Clear all-purpose
adhesive

then cut out, cutting away the tiny circle at the centre as well.

For each king, curve a piece of buckram into a cone and stick, overlapping 2 ins. (see diagram *a*). Cut a piece of foil paper the same shape as the buckram, and stick round the cone.

Fold a napkin in half and cut a 10-in.-diameter semi-circle in *double* paper (straight edge along the fold). Coat one side of this thickly with wallpaper paste, then match centre of straight edge to tip of back of cone, drape round and back as illustrated. When suitably arranged, leave till dry (making sure the pasted cloak doesn't stick to the surface on which the figure is standing).

Wedge a cocktail stick or piece of pipe cleaner into the wooden ball, then lower into the top of the cone and fix inside with a piece of adhesive tape. Make beards by winding knitting wool (not too thick) round two fingertips about ten times: tie the loops very loosely, then stick top to lower part of face, as shown. Or use cotton wool.

To make the conical head-dress, twist a 4-in.-diameter semi-circle of foil paper into a cone to fit head: stick join and then stick into position on head. Cut a strip of double napkin 4 ins. long by 1¼ ins. wide. Coat both sides thickly with paste, twist at the centre front, then drape round base of cone and join ends at the back. Stick diamanté at centre front.

For the turban, cut a 3-in.-diameter circle of napkin. Paste all round the edge, then stick edge round head, puffing out the centre as shown. Finish with a strip stuck round edge of circle as instructed for the conical head-dress.

For the third king, cut a 3½-in. square of napkin. Paste and drape over head as shown. Then stick a scrap of gilt braid round head for crown (or cut in foil paper).

To make Joseph and Mary, draw a 5-in.-diameter circle on the buckram, with a ½-in.-diameter circle in the centre. Divide in half across the middle, then cut the two sections out, cutting away the tiny circle at the centre as well (diagram *b*).

For each figure, curve a piece of buckram into a cone and stick, overlapping 3 ins. (see diagram *b*). Cut a piece of brown paper the same shape as the buckram and stick round one cone, for Joseph, but leave the plain white buckram as it is, for Mary.

Fold a brown napkin in half and cut an 8-in.-diameter semi-circle in *double* paper as for the kings.

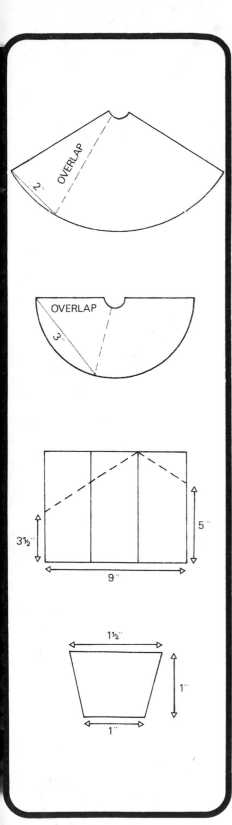

Coat with paste and drape round cone as before. Repeat with a blue napkin for Mary.

Assemble and fix the heads as for the Kings, making Joseph's beard in the same way. Drape a pasted 3-in. square of white napkin over his head, then tie with a scrap of brown raffia, as illustrated. Drape another 5-in.-diameter semi-circle of blue over Mary's head.

Wedge a 2-in. length of cocktail stick into the smaller wooden ball for the Baby Jesus. Pad the stick with cotton wool to form the body, then cut a 6-in.-diameter semi-circle of white napkin, coat thickly with paste and drape round figure as illustrated.

To make the stable, cut the strips of balsa wood into the following pieces:

Base: 1 piece 9 ins. by 3 ins.
       1 piece 9 ins. by 1½ ins.
Back: 3 pieces 7 ins. by 3 ins.
Sides: 1 piece 5 ins. by 3 ins.
       1 piece 3½ ins. by 3 ins.
Roof: 1 piece 9 ins. by 3 ins.
       1 piece 9 ins. by 1½ ins.
       1 piece 6 ins. by 3 ins.
       1 piece 6 ins. by 1½ ins.

Stick the two base pieces edge-to-edge to measure 9 ins. by 4½ ins. Reinforce with tape underneath.

Stick the three back pieces side-by-side, to measure 7 ins. by 9 ins. Cut this piece as indicated by the broken lines in diagram c.

Stick the edges of the two side pieces to the main surface of the back, level with the side edges and top and bottom. Reinforce joins with tiny pins from behind.

Stick the back and sides on top of the base, level with the back and side edges. Reinforce with pins from underneath.

Stick the roof pieces edge-to-edge to measure 9 ins. by 4½ ins. and 6 ins. by 4½ ins. Hinge these together at the centre with a strip of tape, then place in position on top of walls, overlapping the back slightly: stick and pin securely.

"Thatch" the roof with raffia, saturating the strands with wallpaper paste to hold it in position.

To make the crib, cut two strips of wood 3 ins. by 1 in. for the sides. Cut the two ends as diagram d. Stick the ends between the sides, then fix a strip of wood inside to form the base. Fill with short lengths of raffia, and lay the Baby on top.